Stop Being Someone You're Not

Embracing Your God-Given Identity

By

Dr. Barbara L. Gilliam

Genre: Memoir and More

A wholly owned subsidiary of TBN

Stop Being Someone You're Not: Embracing Your God-Given Identity

Trilogy Christian Publishers A Wholly Owned Subsidiary of Trinity Broadcasting Network

2442 Michelle Drive Tustin, CA 92780

Rights Department, 2442 Michelle Drive, Tustin, CA 92780.

Trilogy Christian Publishing/TBN and colophon are trademarks of Trinity Broadcasting Network.

Cover design by: Grant Swank

For information about special discounts for bulk purchases, please contact Trilogy Christian Publishing.

Trilogy Disclaimer: The views and content expressed in this book are those of the author and may not necessarily reflect the views and doctrine of Trilogy Christian Publishing or the Trinity Broadcasting Network.

Manufactured in the United States of America

10 9 8 7 6 5 4 3 2 1

Library of Congress Cataloging-in-Publication Data is available.

ISBN: 979-8-88738-320-0

E-ISBN: 979-8-88738-321-7

Acknowledgments

Thank You to the Lord Jesus Christ, who, by His blood, allowed me to be forgiven and transformed.

Deep love and gratitude for my husband, who helped make this project possible. His sacrifice and encouragement have been priceless.

Without The Walter Hoving Home, the Teen Challenge Ministry, and the Assemblies of God denomination, I would not be present to share this story.

Thank you to Dr. Jim and Twila Edwards for mentoring me and pouring into my life at Evangel University.

Thank you to Dr. Gordon Fee for modeling to me the humility and love of Jesus.

Thanks to my family and especially my mother, Audrey White-Schuppener, for praying me into the kingdom and loving me through the darkest nights.

Thanks to Dr. Joshua and Dr. Sherilyn Smith for their support and friendship.

And thank you to Ken for providing. You know who you are...

Table of Contents

Introduction...5

Chapter 1: How Did I Get Here?................................9

Chapter 2: When Did It Begin?...............................17

Chapter 3: Living with a Clenched Fist...................29

Chapter 4: Moms Don't Quit...................................41

Chapter 5: Oh, What a Tangled Web We
Weave When First We Practice to Deceive.................57

Chapter 6: Addiction...81

Chapter 7: Choose Life or Death...........................103

Chapter 8: Me, a Pastor?..155

Chapter 9: Prayer Learned.....................................177

Chapter 10: Conclusion...197

Contact Information..206

Endnotes..207

Bibliography..209

Introduction

People are straining to find a life of greater satisfaction and meaning. Desperate to make sense of their existence, they embrace damaging philosophies and lifestyles. As the soul yearns for purpose and a sense of belonging, behavior goes further and further into bizarre practices and beliefs that are far from the only solution. The absence of God in a world gone crazy has resulted in sexual perversion, fixation on self, a lack of a worldview or values, and disregard for human life. The prevalence of evil and human pride has produced chaos, hatred, fear, and only subjective truth.

Each person is uniquely created in the image of God and has immeasurable value and importance to Him. God's foremost desire is that every human being experiences His love and accepts the invitation into His family through the death and resurrection of Jesus Christ. Jesus Christ alone can bring genuine, long-lasting fulfillment and contentment, and He alone helps us make sense of our existence. The utopia we crave in this earthly existence will never be found. The moment we enter heaven for eternity all needs and longings will fall off like ragged, useless clothing. God's stamp of authenticity and uniqueness on our life allows us to live out our greatest created potential. Only humans are challenged by the idea of identity and image. Birds sing and do not question if their performance was perfect or want to be something they are not. Salmon don't cease to swim upstream in order to return to their birthplace to breed because the water is turbulent or because they fear not living up to others' expectations. Humans possess some common traits that make up our humanness, but no two people are the same. Our DNA and personality traits and abilities, to who influenced and molded our beliefs and opinions, contribute to who we are as humans. The world is populated with an incredible diversity of people. Often intrigued by the distinctiveness of every finger print and snowflake, each life is designed with a customized and amazing purpose by the Lord.

This memoir recounts how God pursued me into the darkest places to convey to me His love and my worth. Knowing I was deeply loved by God could not surface until I could accept how God saw me and began to embrace the person He created.

Numerous decisions I made could have killed me or sent me to prison. I'm certain that in the midst of the suffering others inflicted on me and my own bad decisions, God was always with me. Jesus' nail-scarred hands never let go of me. It is unimaginable that Jesus' hands full of unconditional love, righteousness, and power would embrace me. All I could offer Him were frail, filthy hands and a messy, sin-covered life. The blood of people I had destroyed with my words and deeds were dripping from my hands. I was withering away—a crumbling structure of a person created in the image of God who believed she was experiencing her destiny. The innocence and purity had been ripped from my soul very early in life.

Distrust and shame followed me down many dead-end roads. But God did not let my life end in death. Jesus Christ birthed me into the kingdom of God by sacrificing His life on the cross, dying a lonely excruciating death in my place. Jesus was born in an unclean stable and knew about messes from the day of His birth. It is my hope that this collection of real-life stories will offer faith, hope, and love to every reader and encouragement to say "yes" to God's invitation. No matter who you are or where you have been, God is waiting with open arms.

When God created man and woman, He was the only frame of reference they experienced. Only perpetual loving communion and truth nurtured Adam and Eve at all times. It was the perfect life and perfect relationship. Their connection with God and one another was irrevocability damaged when they chose to walk away from their Creator and do the one thing He asked them not to do—to eat of the tree of the knowledge of good and evil. God took the risk of designing humans able to make choices as free moral agents even when that meant rejecting Him. Innocent people suffer because of the brokenness of all human beings and the decisions they make. Whether it's war, rejection, greed, or abuse, God suffers with man in all these areas of choices.

God did not abandon us; we are still marked by the fact we are created in His image. His love does not waver, and He Himself reversed the destiny of every person, paying the price for our forgiveness, redemption, and wholeness.

When I finally responded to God's personal invitation to have a relationship with Him, I came as a severely wounded solider, ready to surrender defeat. My physical body was bruised and haggard, my mind disoriented, and my soul hemorrhaging. In a weak and tired tone, I said to God, "I promise if You get me out of this, I'll clean up my act and go to church." The response was, "You cannot clean up your life, but if you let Me clean up your life, I will transform you into the person you were intended to become."

Accepting our true identity is a gift to be received and is critical in discovering our purpose. Instead of creating a false image that shifts with chameleon-like ease depending on the crowd, God empowered us to discover the authentic person He created. This discovery is an ongoing process of letting go of who we thought we were and sought to be, replaced by the identity God gave us. It is an adventurous journey with heavenly realities and purposes made real in our daily lives. The roots of our pretend self-lie in our childhood discovery that we can secure love by presenting ourselves as we think others want us. "We become so self-deceived that we strive to maintain the delusion of the person we think see in the mirror. God wants a person to know the self that he knows; the good, the bad, and the ugly."[i]

Chapter 1:
How Did I Get Here?

I heard the keys as she came down the hall; opening the small window on the door, she shouted, "How are you doing?" Her disconnected glare stared through me as though I wasn't there. Shrugging my shoulders, I answered, "Okay, I guess." She quickly disappeared with her pocket of keys. As I gazed out of the thickly screened window, the words of the judge blared in my mind, *You are to be turned over to the board of control to be institutionalized at Mitchellville Training School for Girls. Trained for what?* I thought. Mitchellville had a scandalous reputation and had been compared to a prisoner-of-war camp. At fifteen I didn't have the ability or perspective to understand how and why our family was fragmented. The abuse I experienced at the hands of my father was buried deeply under the debris of broken pieces of identity.

After parking near the main office of Mitchellville, the car stopped, and the two probation officers and the pastor who was at my court hearing two days earlier got out. We entered the office of the administrator, who was an older attractive woman. She stood erect and proper and smiled as she welcomed me. After the probation officers and pastor left, the administrator told me several rules I needed to respect, which would determine some of my progress. Afterward I was taken to a building that housed isolation rooms called "the hospital." Greeting me was a short, pudgy, poker-faced nurse dressed in white. She handed me a liquid to kill lice and other bugs and escorted me to the showers. "Don't forget to wash your private parts," she muttered. After the shower I was told to put on a gown that felt like burlap and wasn't allowed underwear. She ushered me to a small isolated room and locked the door behind me. I sat on the flimsy bed and fought erupting tears. I told myself I had to gain self-control and not allow others to see me as weak or vulnerable. Fighting between the girls and abuse by officers discredited the reputation of the institution. I took a deep breath and wiped my tears with the back of my hand.

My probation officer, letters from teachers, and the pastor witnessed at my hearing. The final incident that brought me to court was walking into an unlocked house and stealing a bottle of whiskey. Each one testified that I was a troubled juvenile delinquent, though I don't recall ever having more than a five-minute conversation with any of them. I was never asked a question about my life, though my behavior had gotten me to this place. Especially hurtful were the statements the pastor made on my behalf, "I've known this girl since she was a baby. I baptized her and confirmed her in the teachings of the Lutheran Church. Her family is in good standing with the congregation of St. Stephens. I'm afraid if she isn't placed in a state facility, she will end up dead and bloody in an alley." He didn't have a clue who I was, and I'd never truly had a conversation with him. We were members of the church in name only. Mom was the only one in the family he liked and interacted with. I think he felt sorry for Mom, a strong and steadfast Norwegian wife and mother who played the organ during services and mimeographed the church bulletins every week. I recall several years later Mom saying that on at least one occasion she asked the pastor to counsel our family, but sadly he told her he did not know how. I found him distant and self-righteous, and I never understood what he believed. When he spoke those words in court that day, I turned to him with complete rage and disgust and said, "You can take my membership and burn the logs in your @@### fireplace, you @@###! Because of you, I'll never step foot in a church again!"

Right after sentencing, two uniformed police officers each grabbed an arm, directing me to the exit. Mom was crying out, "Don't take my daughter away." Entering the elevator, I cursed God and let Him know how much I hated Him! I also hated myself; afflicted with shame and worthlessness, I wanted to die. I was put directly in jail and would be driven to Mitchellville the following morning. As days passed I adapted to the daily routine. Though uncertain how long I had been there, the leaves were slowly dancing to the ground from the maple tree at the center of the campus.

One evening around six, the guard was instructing us to line up and return to our rooms; I saw a dark blue Chevy slowly rounding the corner on the road next to our cottage. Like a magnet pulling me, I picked a blade of grass, put it in my mouth, and started walking toward the car. Knowing I'd suffer drastic consequences, I continued toward it as the car slowed down. I squinted as I strained to see who was driving while the house mother screamed, "Get back here now." A woman with dark hair was driving, but I did not recognize her. Suddenly her index finger motioned for me to come to her. My legs started to run toward the car like a jack rabbit fleeing a fire, and when I reached the car, she flung open the back door. I dove in the back, and with the smell of burning rubber, we took off. Another car was blocking our exit, so with a quick turn, we detoured through the garden. Tomato plants flew up in the air as the car dug deep into the ground. As we entered a gravel road, I hopped in the front seat and realized the person driving needed a shave! As I looked closer, I pulled off the wig and discovered it wasn't a woman; it was my father! "Get the @@## out of here!" I shouted as the smell of bourbon strongly permeated the car. Dad turned onto a highway that led us to Des Moines, a city large enough to hide in.

I believe the Lord drew me to the car that night. Though most people would respond by saying escaping was a crime and God wouldn't condone someone committing a crime. Due to the verbal and physical abuse I witnessed at Mitchellville, I believe God wanted all the girls and me out of there.

The goal of the staff at Mitchellville was to "make nice young women" of us. Many of the rules, like not being allowed to cross your legs or being banned from talking during meals, further restricted conversation. They used the girls to work jobs that should have been delegated to experienced adults. I was made to scrape paint off the walls of a large room that was not being used. Paint chips fell on my eyelashes and hair, and I was subjected to toxic chemicals. After that job was complete, I had to clean the wood floor and use a buffer that was noisy to a degree. Slightly humming under my breath seemed to ease some stress as I worked on the room. Miss Kirk, the woman in charge of that project, walked up to me while I was on my hands and knees cleaning the floor. "What are you humming for?" she asked. All I saw as I looked up were two old black shoes that reminded me of what the two crazy old ladies wore in the movie *Arsenic and Old Lace.* "I'm just humming." "Well, stop it; it's very annoying," she said firmly. As she walked away, she shouted, "Make sure this floor is spic and span and buffed well."

On another occasion I spent five days in lock up for writing to my boyfriend. Knowing getting a letter out of the facility was not possible, putting on paper how I felt seemed to ease my frustration. As I was being released to return to the cottage, I passed the office where a young twelve-year-old girl was crying and frightened because she had swallowed a pin during sowing class. Her room was across the hall from me. The same gruff-sounding nurse who had no understanding or empathy for the girls began to slap her and screamed repeatedly, "Why did you put that pin in your mouth?" As if in slow motion, I watched myself begin to lunge at the woman, fully prepared to kill her. Something stopped me, and I believe it was God. But I discovered I was capable of murder or severely injuring that nurse. Other physical and emotional abuse, some of which I experienced, triggered the rage that was concealed in a deep internal graveyard but was not dead. The actions of the staff and leadership of this institution were not only illegal but immoral and cruel. Hadn't these girls experienced enough mistreatment and shame?

The night Dad got me out, the police immediately put out an all-points bulletin reporting that a woman illegally entered the grounds

13

in order to provide a means for me to escape. Mom was working as a private duty nurse and knew nothing about my disappearance. Dad decided we needed to leave Iowa and so we caught the last flight to Chicago. Taking a taxi to downtown Chicago, I was captivated by the traffic, the tall buildings, and the flashing lights. "Here's your hotel, sir," the driver pulled up to the front entrance of the Drake Hotel. As we entered the busy lobby, I felt relatively safe from anyone who knew us. But our odd appearance could draw concern. Dad still had eye makeup on from the getaway; I had the old fashion clothes from the institution, and we had no luggage. We checked in to a room with a queen size bed, and both plopped down on the bed with a sigh. Almost immediately, we went and bought a couple of pieces of clothes and toiletries for each of us. In the busy sidewalks, I became paranoid, wondering what I'd do if a policeman grabbed my arm. At the hotel Dad and I devised a plan. If law enforcement came to the door, he would hand me the $1,000 cash, and I was to take off as he hit the person.

After dinner, I held my breath as dad picked up a pay phone and called Mom. When she asked to talk with me, I was gulping down breaths to stay quiet as I took the phone and let out a big sigh. "It's so good to hear your voice, Mom. I'm sorry you didn't know about this. I didn't know either. But we're okay, and I know I'll see you soon." No matter what, I always found myself protecting Mom. Even at a young age, I understood this hard-working, loving woman didn't deserve all the pain she'd experienced in our family. I didn't understand the magnitude of why I felt so protective of Mom until years later. In the following days, we rendezvoused with Mom in a small Illinois town. She drove our Ford Falcon to meet us and took a bus home. I ran to her with open arms when she pulled up. As we ate lunch at a local diner, Dad described in detail how he got me out. Mom said the police came to the house, and she believed they were watching who came and went. Her goal was to sell the house and get out of Iowa once we got settled somewhere. I hated to see her go, but before she got on the bus, we stopped at the local Dairy Queen, where we laughed and enjoyed our favorite treat of chocolate dilly bars. Dad decided we should head south until we landed in a safe place.

On day two of travel, we drove through a thunderstorm south of St. Louis. The worn-out windshield wipers scraped against the windshield, causing a rhythmical sound that helped me relax. I looked out the window and asked myself how I got to this place; the answer wasn't far away. Mesmerized by the rain, I began to review my young life. Leaning against the passenger side window, I viewed a mental slide show of the events of my young life.

Chapter 2:

When Did It Begin?

At age seven my personality changed from a shy, innocent girl to an aggressive, unruly child. On the school playground, I began to bully boys, yelling and hitting them. In the classroom I refused to listen to my math and physical education teacher, Mr. Ferguson. By ages eight and nine, I was vandalizing property and calling in false fires or bombs. What compels a child to do these acts? Was it boredom or the thrill of hearing the emergency vehicles or watching people react? Years later, I realized there was an emergency because my house was on fire and I needed to be rescued; I just didn't know how to ask for help.

"If you want to know how emotionally stable a girl is, try asking about her dad. A father-daughter relationship is a key to a woman's happiness and life."

A daughter needs a dad to be the standard against which she will judge all men.

It started on a Sunday afternoon after lunch. I was four. Dad was a photographer, among other talents, and asked me to be his model.

Dad picked me up and sat me on his photography bench. "You want to be my model?" he asked me.

"Yes, I can learn to model really good," I answered. What four-year-old daughter would not want to be her dad's model? My dad thought I was pretty enough and talented enough at such a young age. He had faith I could do it, and I felt so special. I was as proud as a four-year-old little girl could be. "When do we start? When do we start?" I asked every day until a Sunday afternoon we'd just finished the Swiss steak, mashed potatoes, green beans, and cookies Grandma made every Sunday. When the clanging of the pots and dishes started, I walked over to our apartment next door.

Dad peaked his head around to door and asked, "You want to model for me today?"

"Oh yes!" I dressed up in my lightly flowered dress with yellow and blue flowers and a large pink belt that tied in a bow in the front. I had to wear my black patent shoes with a strap across the middle and my fancy white socks. A white bow in my hair finished my wardrobe. I felt as beautiful inside as I felt on the outside. With innocence and trust, I grabbed onto Dad as he lifted me onto a table covered with fabric. I was to sit on the edge and cross my legs. I felt like a beautiful innocent princess who was worthy of love. He handed me one of Mom's cups and saucer, and I would pose and pretend I was drinking coffee. He arranged the bottom of my dress so it was like an open fan. Dad took lots of shots that day of me in various positions. When we were done, he turned on the music, and I stood on his feet as we danced.

By age five, the erosion of trust and predictability was fragmenting our family. The amount and frequency of Dad's drinking increased, substituting his time with his family to drink and caress other women. When he was home, we all wished he was gone. Dad became verbally abusive, and late-night arguments with Mom were commonplace. He was a handsome man who loved entertaining people and being admired by everyone, especially women. He was a proficient musician on the piano and was in demand in bars and clubs. When Dad was home, he occasionally prepared gourmet-style meals like beef stroganoff or spaghetti and meatballs.

He disregarded most of the rules, not hesitating to lie and make his own guidelines as he went.

Dad started to molest me when I was six. He whispered to me that I would always be his model and that I was so beautiful. He raped me that night. It was the beginning of my innocence being ripped from my soul. Within the year, I had become an angry, defiant child, and the abuse continued for the next three to four years.

The smell of alcohol and chewing tobacco woke me as Dad climbed into bed. Dad's mental and spiritual health worsened, and by the following year, he was spending more time with a group of younger guys he met at bars. Eventually, he seduced them into believing in his latest project that he originated from a place called Plant X. One of the guys was a skinny hyper man named Kenny the Prophet. Kenny believed he could leave his body and visit other locations and that he had powers to curse people. As the group grew and they got deeper into the occult, I was offered to the men in the group. They said I needed to be "seeded" by Dad and the others so I could have access to Planet X also. A crushing sense of evil and darkness fastened around me every time I was present with Dad and his followers. Every aspect of my life was affected by the abuse and madness.

"Barbara, I want to talk to you," Mr. Ferguson, the math teacher in my fifth-grade class, said firmly. He put his hand on my neck and guided me to an empty classroom. "Sit down. I'm asking you why you are so cruel to Charles and others. Why are you constantly getting in trouble?"

I gave him a blank stare, looked away, and said, "I don't know."

"Okay, you can go back to class."

The teachers and administration didn't know what action to take or suspected life was that bad at home. Dad had a reputation of being a drunk and a womanizer.

Life became more frenzied at home. My brother had nightmares and would come into my room at night saying things that made no sense. Days or nights left at home alone with my brother and father activated panic and a sense of being powerless. Feeling so desperate one day, I dialed the operator and asked if she could help me. Without telling her why I needed help, she directed me to call my parents. At age twelve I was taken to a social worker who advised my parents to not leave me alone, as she felt I was suicidal. The next day, my dad was "watching me" and said, "Are you going to bump yourself off or what? I got a lot of work to do." Obviously, I survived. We just laughed it off, always using humor as a defense and as a means of avoiding the sadness and secrets in our life.

"Sad is the life of the woman who asks for love and instead gets passion."

Passion or Love

Passion is a state of being. It is a temporary level of total ecstasy and pleasure. It is about what feels good and focused on self-gratification. Though passion is part of a loving marriage relationship, it is not the basis for love. I learned later that Dad was a true narcissist who believed the world must evolve around him.

> Pleasure is like light; if you grab at it, you miss it; if you try to bottle it, you get only darkness; if you let it pass, you catch the glory. The self has a built-in, God-imaging design of self-fulfillment by self-forgetfulness, pleasure through unselfishness, ecstasy by *ekstasis*, "standing-out-side-the-self."[ii]

God's love is everlasting and frees us to receive the gift of unconditional love and acceptance. Striving to live up to a certain standard or level of performance for the Lord to love me is not necessary. Love allows the other person to choose and doesn't take their freedom or ability to make choices. Using power manipulation to control someone can be camouflaged with words, gifts, or promises. Freedom without responsibility or respect caused me to be held captive by power and passion, not love. God's love does not have an agenda with impure or hidden motives to harm anyone. A woman who has been violated generally continues to be sexually promiscuous and is riddled with shame and disgust. Drugs or alcohol become the numbing agent that allows a person to sustain oneself. Fear of abandonment can incite a person to engage in behaviors that betray the person's beliefs and values. Feeling internally empty and forsaken, the heart cries out for legitimate and unqualified love. The obsession with being unconditionally loved can dictate decisions and conduct. Believing at a young age that love is painful and conditional, the endgame becomes avoiding rejection by doing what everyone wants. Trust is an essential part of a person's life and is for any level of intimacy or closeness. Purpose and direction are severely skewed when a person does not trust self. Accepting the truth that a person is made in the image of God is challenging when shame and degradations hide the real person.

It has taken years to work on forgiving my father and myself from the early sexual abuse. Shame and self-blame create a negative view of self as worthless and partially responsible for the assaults. The realization that I am made in God's image and I bear His identity in my own unique way is God's design and desire.

After watching the episodes of my life pass through my vision like the review of an old film, I suddenly returned to the present and saw that we were driving in the Smoky Mountains. It was surreal that I had actually escaped the institution where I'd been committed by the state of Iowa. It was still raining when we reached Louisville, Kentucky, so we had dinner and stayed the night. Feeling as though I was still in a dreamlike state, I had to talk to Mom. Dad said he was going to get cigarettes, but I knew he would buy a bottle of liquor or wine. I briefly talked to Mom while he was gone. After he was sleeping, I quietly pulled out the bottle of bourbon from under the bathroom sink and gagged down two gulps. Pulling back my head, I thought I'd burned my throat. In a few moments, I was more relaxed and watched an episode of *Gilligan's Island* while eating Cheetos. Though I swore I would never become an alcoholic like him, I did savor temporary feelings of tranquility and confidence. Experiences that demand more resources for coping than a person perceives they possess can cause a trauma that upsets that person's capacity to handle psychological needs.

Escaping Mitchellville brought certain relief and hope, but I still sought to ease the internal pain and confusion using mood-altering chemicals. The sense of euphoria that drugs provided was fleeting, and the chore of continually seeking painkillers was exhausting. When encountering the gaping pain inside, relief was all I sought. Assuming that I was a weak-willed person was coupled with the belief I had a diminished intellectual capacity and no true moral convictions.

An assortment of drugs, alcohol, and other numbing agents would become the remedy for a life that couldn't rest with the person I had become. After years of deadening the pain receptors, denial and self-deception afflicted me like a person with leprosy of the soul. While under the influence of these false, double-crossing chemicals, I felt life was tolerable. Evidently the chemicals turn on you and become your enemy, causing extensive denial and deception. Through the years, I began to believe that the woman in the mirror was not the misled person I had become but a presentable lady that was wise and could have the life she desired. Minimizing leads to denial, which eventually results in a life crisis. It is certainly insanity when a person who has been deluded by addiction views what he or she wants to see instead of reality. At that point, chemicals or behaviors have become the god we worship, and Satan works to continue the façade and deception.

Insight: Is there a time in your life you were looking for love and instead were given passion or abuse? Who has loved you for who you are and restored the fact that you are a valuable person?

I needed some form of dignity and sacredness to be restored to my body and soul. How could I ever live as a person created in the *imago Dei* (image of God)? Believing that God viewed me from the lens of a discarded, unclean woman, I doubted the power and extent of His love.

We drifted to Florida, where we rented an efficiency apartment in Fort Lauderdale by the sea. A Jewish couple and their mother owned and operated the four-unit apartments. It took only weeks until Dad located an old girlfriend in town near us. Meanwhile, Marilyn, the owner of the apartments, and her mother, Grandma Yosen, treated me like a daughter. As only a Coney Island New Yorker could say, Grandma Yosen told me daily as she took a puff on her Benson and Hedges cigarette, "Barbara, darling, just remember that it's just as easy to marry a rich man as a poor man. Do yourself a favor and make sure you marry a guy with money or at least a sugar daddy that will take good care of you." She only fed the belief that had been in my heart for a long time. I did not realize until years later that I just wanted to be taken care of. The little girl inside was crying out for love and safety.

Combing his hair and dressed in his best suit, Dad said:

"Barb, I'm going to meet with an old friend of mine from Iowa. I went to school with her, and we haven't talked in years. I'll be home about midnight."

"Okay, leave me a couple of bucks in case I need something."

Dad handed me a $20.00 dollar bill. Days passed with no word from Dad. Finally, after over a week, he walked in the door. It looked like he'd slept in his suit and the rest of him looked disheveled. I could smell alcohol seeping through his skin. Distracted by putting clothes away, I said:

"Thankful that Marilyn and her family and Grandma Yosen looked after me, Dad. Why didn't you call me?"

"I did call, Barb, and left a message with Julie (Marilyn's young daughter). I gave her Pat's number and said to have you call me."

"I never got the message. So who is this woman?"

"She's a very wealthy woman I went to high school with and dated for a while. I'd like you to meet her."

"Why?"

"She'd like to meet you."

"Does she want to meet Mom too? Is she an alcoholic like you?" There was silence, and Dad went to take a shower.

I enrolled in night school to obtain my GED. Marilyn drove me to class for the first two weeks. It was about 10:00 a.m. on a Tuesday morning when I started walking around the area. The fan leaves on the tall palm trees lifted slightly as a pleasant breeze promised to cool down the asphalt streets. Most of the houses looked like bungalows with jalousie windows that resembled Venetian blinds. I approached a small strip mall, where I saw small specialty shops and a large cafeteria. I walked to the door of the cafeteria, and though they weren't open for business, the door wasn't locked, so I walked in.

A young man with a number of assorted keys dangling from his belt approached me. "Can I help you?" he smiled.

"Do you need help?" I asked.

25

"Follow me to the office, and I'll give you an application."

Though it was a risk, I put my correct name on the job application. After a short interview, I was hired. I could walk there, and my hours didn't interfere with night classes. Maybe I could make a fresh start here; maybe I could straighten out my life.

I started working at the cafeteria while taking classes. Mom finally left Iowa and came to live with us. Being a private-duty registered nurse, Mom worked long hours to support the family. Dad spent money on every get-rich-quick scheme. Through the years, Mom started divorce proceedings due to Dad's alcoholism and infidelity, but she always gave it one more try. Soon after Mom arrived in Florida, we got another apartment, and she finally filed for divorce.

After obtaining my GED and working in a cafeteria, I got a job at a travel agency. The owner was an older man whose son, Dale, a widower, managed the agency. Soon I was asked if I wanted to go on a free trip that the travel agency called a familiarization trip. Airlines and hotels offered it complimentary as a marketing tool. A group of fifteen of us from various agencies met at Fort Lauderdale Airport and boarded for St. Thomas in the Virgin Islands. The alcohol was flowing before we reached thirty-two thousand feet. I didn't refuse a drop of alcohol, danced, and partied. Travel agents were guzzlers, and the party never stopped. Dale was from Wisconsin, and he and his two sons had moved to Florida eight years earlier to help his father and mother. He was a decent man with traditional values and a good work ethic. His wife had died of cancer fifteen years ago, and he was raising his two sons. Within months I introduced Mom to him at an event for the agency. Dale and Mom attended the same Presbyterian Church, and after months of cordial smiles and greetings, Dale asked her to attend a travel agency party on a ship one Friday evening. After a small number of other outings together, Dale and Mom were practically inseparable. It was common for Dale to cook on the grill at his apartment, and we would bring the side dishes. Close to seven years later, I was elated to hear that Dale and Mom were getting married. A sense of blissful peace filled me knowing Dale would care and provide for Mom.

Chapter 3:

Living with a Clenched Fist

"Fools give full vent to their rage, but the wise bring calm in the end" (Proverbs 29:11, NIV).

Smoking cigarettes strengthened the callus exterior I wanted others to see. It wasn't unusual to steal them from home or the store by age ten. My neighbor Jeannie was eleven, and she could smoke in front of her stepmother, which I deemed true freedom. Jeannie lived next door with her eight siblings, and each went to Catholic school, so I saw her mostly on weekends. One Saturday afternoon, we were walking on the railroad tracks throwing rocks at the freight cars and talking about the latest trends in haircuts. We decided to walk home by the old steam engine that stood on display at the end of the tracks. The engine was a meeting place for kids and fun to explore, and though we'd been on it lots of times, we climbed up the stairs to where the engineer sat. We heard laughing in the rear of the car; two older boys goofing around. The boys started walking to the front where we sat. They told us to get up and let them sit there; I told them, "Go to ##!" I recognized one of the boys, Melvin, from the neighborhood. The other kid, Donald, pulled my hair and said:

"What did you say?"

"I said go to @##!"

Jeannie and I made a jump for the stairs, but both boys grabbed us and started to fondle our breasts. When Melvin tore my shirt, something exploded inside, and I pushed him down the stairs. He

29

hit his head on the gravel pathway and didn't move. Jeannie and I ran while his friend yelled at Melvin to get up, but he didn't move. Out of breath from running, I said, "Do you think he's dead?" "I don't know." That night I called the two hospitals, but Melvin wasn't there. I hardly slept, and early the next day, I ran to the drug store to buy a newspaper, certain I'd see Melvin's death on the front page. I was almost at the end of the alley when the two boys came around the corner and pushed me against the wall. "You thought you hurt me, you little @@!!#." Melvin pulled a knife and put it to my throat. "We laughed watching you two run." Without notice someone grabbed Melvin's collar and pulled him to the ground; it was Jerry, the boy across the street who barely spoke to anyone. He punched Melvin and kicked him in the ribs and warned him he better never see his face around again. Melvin limped away like a wounded tiger. I thanked Jerry and asked if I could buy him a soda. He smiled and said, "Am okay; are you?" "I'm fine." "Take care," he mumbled as he walked away. Why was Jerry so shy? Why didn't he look at me when I talked to him? I never saw him with friends or at school.

Sitting in the principal's office the next Tuesday after recess, I could hear him talking to the playground teacher. She walked by me while his finger motioned for me to enter his office. "Why did you hit Matthew in the stomach and take his ball, Barbara?" he asked. "I hit him because he wouldn't let me play the game with him." "That is no reason to hit him and take the ball. Is there anything you want to tell me? Why are you constantly picking fights with people on the playground?" "No reason," I said. I knew what was about to happen when he walked to the door and asked his secretary to come in the office. My stomach tightened as he told me to bend over the chair and took his paddle from his drawer. I felt the wind as he drew back the swatter. Closing my eyes, I heard a piercing sound as the wood connected to my body. Feeling as though I'd been electrocuted, the pain rippled down my legs. Refusing to show any emotion, I stood up expressionless as he told me to back to class. I was also assigned 500 dictionary words to write after school that day and to apologize in front of the teacher to Matthew. I completed my punishment, but I remained unaffected.

A Bully among Us

Bulling kids brought temporary feelings of power and control. An attempt to domineer others was my desperation to steal a person's power and control. Feeling powerless and trapped resulted from abuse and chaos at home. Unexpressed rage piled up inside like stacks of logs ready for the fireplace on a cold night. Not able to find an outlet to express feelings and facts, I chose to cause others pain. Whispering cruel words in the ear of the timid young man sitting in front of me in class was one avenue of expression. People, especially children, who are hurting, cause others to hurt. Somewhere in my mind, I believed hitting and kicking kids and bullying them could shield me from further pain and offer me a sense of control. Chronic young victims explode outwardly instead of imploding. I didn't understand why I found satisfaction in bullying others. Sensing and making fun of their liabilities or disabilities, whether a person's speech, how they dressed, or having a sheepish personality, triggered a sense of power and control. Many years later, as an older adult, I was able to apologize to Charles, a boy I poked fun at numerous times. I'd thought and prayed for him through the years, and a picture was fixed in my mind of tears flowing down Charles' face as he left the classroom because I tortured the poor boy with words that hurt. I don't recall what I said, but I'm grateful I had the opportunity to ask him for forgiveness some fifty years later. Charles said he didn't really remember the incidents but was willing to forgive me anyway.

In fifth grade I thought Keith was the cutest boy I'd ever seen. His crew-cut blonde hair and rosy cheeks drew me to him. He smiled, and it felt like he was a happy kid. He had a list of the girls he liked, and I was always second to my friend Linda. One day after school, Keith was walking near my house in the football field. We walked around the field, and then I told Keith I wanted to be first on his girlfriend list and said to kiss me. I couldn't stop staring at his crispy-clean-looking face and luminous blue eyes. His blonde crew-cut style hair and wide smile caused me to follow him like a starving puppy dog. Keith didn't seem to mind and laughed at my proposal to give me another half point closer to being his number-one girlfriend. I tripped him, and as he was lying on his back, I sat on his stomach, held his arms with my legs, and said, "You can't get up until you kiss me." His carefree, hearty laughter caused me to laugh as I leaned forward to kiss his moist lips. I let him up, and we laughed as we walked back to the school.

I was skilled at most sports and surpassed several boys my age at basketball and the fifty-yard dash. Sports were a constructive means of letting out anger. My tough exterior kept some people at a distance, though I was yearning for closeness and acceptance. Smoking cigarettes, shoplifting, and drinking alcohol brought short spurts of relief, but underlying rage reared its venomous head when least expected like an unannounced snake coiled and ready to attack. Anger was an active volcano bubbling in the background and explosive and misguided. I attempted to avoid the minefields in my mind, heart, and soul. I was manipulated and used, feeling condemned and self-contempt for not stopping such horror. Though studies conclude that a young girl can do little to stop a family member from abuse amid threats, the giving of generous gifts and false promises complicated my reasoning.

Experiencing life with a growing contaminated mind and a hardened heart, peace and a sense of safety slowly slipped away. Hypervigilance or sensory sensitivity manifests as a result of abuse, especially in children. A person who is hypervigilant is in a continual state of alertness and extremely sensitive to surroundings. Substances and remaining in the middle of the circle of strong people provided peaceful moments. Anger and resentment reinforce a cold and armored heart. Anger and fear have a similar biological response that stimulates the body to secrete adrenalin, which is a fight-or-flight hormone, producing additional strength and energy. Both anger and fear produce higher blood pressure; sometimes the body stiffs, and the heartbeat increases. It felt easier to be angry than fearful, though both turned inward become depression. Anger and rage intensify feelings of loss of control and powerlessness.

Stuffing anger or resentment does not eliminate the feelings but is a heavy burden that affects the entire person. A myriad of Christians who don't truly know what the Bible says believe it is unchristian to be angry. Jesus provided several scriptures on the contrary. Probably the popular passage often quoted is found in Ephesians 4:26 (NIV), where Paul states, "In your anger do not sin. Do not let the sun go down while you are still angry." The church is filled with angry, nice people who have not learned how to address their anger other than by praying. Prayer is a pivotal act in the process of understanding and resolving anger. But prayer is not always the only means of settling the feelings and causes of anger or resentment.

When a person doesn't apologize for something he or she did or said to you, it remains necessary for you to forgive the person anyway. Unresolved hostility and resentment make it impossible for a free and loving life.

Sitting on the porch, I was asking myself what it was about this kid Jerry. Why did I feel safe when I saw him? Perhaps I sensed that Jerry had survived much in his young life also. In the back of my mind was a desire to know more about him. Weeks later, I was riding my bike by the Dairy Queen when Jerry turned from the window holding a large vanilla ice cream cone. I quickly stopped, got off my bike, and pretended I was in line. Jerry sat at a picnic bench under the spacious old oak tree. I had no money but just stood there as though I was undecided about what frosty treat to order. I turned around, smiled at him, and got back on my bike, riding slowly past where he sat.

"Hi," I said as I stopped.

"Hey," he nodded. "How's it going?" he asked.

That's all it took to give me a reason to go sit at the bench. "I'm good, just always in trouble for fighting or doing something stupid." "I heard you liked to cause trouble," he said with a smile. Surprised by his next question, I said nothing.

"How come you act like that?" he asked. "It can mess your life up for good, and you can't take it back. I know," he continued.

"Why? What did you ever do?" I asked.

"Up until two years ago, I lived with my mom, my three younger sisters, and my stepfather. After Mom married him, life drastically changed. He was a cruel, nasty man and beat my sisters and me regularly. The most heartbreaking for me and my sisters is that my mom didn't defend us. He was her third husband. She worked as a butcher at the local Kikes Market and had a better job than he did; I don't know why she married the guy. I resented him, and I let hatred grow; then one night after he beat all three of my sisters, it's like I went into a rage. I knew where he kept the gun he used when he worked as an auxiliary cop at events. I pulled it out of the container, made sure there were bullets in there, and went up to him and said to his face, 'You will never touch me or my sisters again.' Then I pulled the trigger and shot him in the face. I dropped the gun and ran out the door. I just kept running and running until I got to a friend's house. I didn't know his parents were home, but I knocked on the door, and Jake answered. I motioned for him to come on the porch and told him what I had done. 'Jerry, you're in trouble. I know he was a cold, mean guy, but you better come in.' His parents called the police, and I was taken to juvenile hall. My mom came to see me in jail, but I refused. My court date was a week later, and my friend's parents hired a lawyer for me. For some reason Jake's parents believed in giving me a chance; they believed in me. People testified about the abuse, and what hurt me the most was to watch my sisters take the stand and describe the beatings."

I interrupted, "Did he die, Jerry...did your stepdad die?"

"No, fortunately he lived but has had several surgeries to his throat and face. My mom divorced him, and she and my sisters started going to a counselor. I got a year in juvenile jail and two years of counseling. I was paroled last year to a step house for boys, where I'm living now. I'm glad he lived because I wouldn't be talking to you now if he died. I have regrets, but nothing like I'd have if I'd killed him. I've learned to communicate more, to respond and not react. I know what it's like to feel afraid and powerless. I'm saying this to you because you need to talk to someone, Barbara, about what is going on in your house and in you. Your brother has told me some details of the craziness. If you don't talk to someone, you may do something that will haunt you the rest of your life. I can tell you've been hurt and you're angry, but deep down, you're just a hurt little girl who wants to be cared for and loved. That sounds weird coming from a guy like me, but I've watched my sisters and mom forgive each other and make healthier choices. I've decided to go back to school and become a social worker for delinquent children and their families. We also started going to church together, and the youth pastor has been an understanding friend and someone I can depend on. I'm still figuring God out and why He let all this crap happen, but I think we are better today than ever." Jerry smiled and said, "Come on, I'll buy you a cone." That day changed my life.

In the days following, I started to question if I was meant to be a boy or a girl. I wasn't like the typical girl in my class who liked the latest fashions or prematurely wore a bra. Why did I like wearing pants and practicing fighting and boxing? I excelled at most sports and could tackle any guy in my school wearing a full football uniform. It wouldn't be until years later I realized I wanted to project the image of a gangster or bully so men wouldn't rape me again. I felt awkward about being feminine, but I knew I didn't want to be with girls. Asking myself what it meant to be feminine and what that looked like, I realized my only model was my mother. Feeling shame and lack of confidence, I expressed my sexuality in a self-destructive cycle of drug and alcohol abuse, which allowed me to sell myself to men. At that point, I hated men and desired from them all the material and financial possessions I could grab.

As I continued to portray a tough exterior, rage and depression were concealed in the dark corners of my heart. "Barbara, you remind me of Calamity Jane." Those words were spoken to me by a captain in the Cedar Rapids Police Department after several confrontations I had with the police. Having no hint of who Calamity Jane was, I investigated the woman several years later. Calamity Jane was a woman of the Wild West, renowned for her skill with guns and horses. She lived hard and wild. Drinking whiskey fortified her tough exterior, and at times she would fight even the most dominant and experienced Indian fighter. Her parents died when she was twelve, and she cared for herself by any means necessary. Jane appeared in the Buffalo Bill's Wild West Shows around the country featuring her riding and shooting skills. Her chronic drunkenness and fighting caused her to be fired, and she retired to Deadwood, South Dakota, where rumor has it she had a romantic relationship with the gambler and gunslinger Wild Bill Hickok. Calamity Jane died in a hotel room from pneumonia and alcoholism. Being compared to Calamity Jane was a compliment at first, but not long after reading about her tragic life, I resolved to shed that image.

When my behavior or speech were way out of line, my mom or grandmother would tightly grab my shoulders and say, "Who do you think you are?" I was looking to them to tell me who I was or should aspire to become. Why couldn't I act like a civilized person? Observing the "smart" and well-liked kids in school, I thought it seemed natural and simple for them to apply themselves to study and good behavior. Neurological and organic brain diseases like autism and attention deficit disorders were not known or at least not considered when evaluating a child's behavior. The inner workings of a child's development and environmental influences did not appear to be a consideration during these turbulent years.

As I lived with my hands in fight mode most of the time, it became clear that a person cannot receive anything positive if you live with clenched fists, nor can you let go of toxic, unwanted influences. Not until I put my arms down and let my hands unfold to relax could my hands open to receive from the Lord and others. Blinded by unworthiness and chaos, I was oblivious to values I held that disappeared years ago. Would I ever know dignity and grace again in my life? Perhaps the form of unfaithfulness is betraying self. A close disciple of Jesus named Judas betrayed Jesus for little more than loose coins. He kissed Jesus on the cheek to identify him as the man the authorities sought. It states in Matthew 27:3 (NIV) that later Judas was "seized with remorse, returned the thirty pieces of silver he received for turning Jesus in to the officials, and then went away and hanged himself."

"To thine own self be true" becomes increasingly significant as a person ages. Self-betrayal is an enormously high price to pay that blocks inner peace and the final particle of self-worth.

Insight: Is there a time in your life when you betrayed yourself? Describe what was going on at that time and how you have recaptured your fidelity. Who helped you to recapture your dignity and self-worth?

Chapter 4:

Moms Don't Quit

The first breath of life is followed by loud crying, which indicates life. Born on a cold Iowa on the 4th of July was an indication of how riveting my life would be. My brother, Greg, was eighteen months older, and his sensitivity to milk and overly stimulated nervous system required a large portion of both parents' attention and care. My first home was in a bassinet in the kitchen of our tiny apartment. Our apartment was in the large house my fraternal grandmother owned. A small bathroom separated our apartment. She was a short, hefty woman whose large breasts got to the room before the rest of her. Grandma was a hard worker and spent many of her years as the housekeeping manager of a large apartment/hotel a few blocks from home. Grandma never lost her Scottish brogue and walked around her apartment singing Scottish songs. Knocking before entering or asking permission to enter the apartment never happened. It was too easy to walk in with such a short distance separating us and Grandma's need to control circumstances and people. Her husband died in a gardening accident when she was quite young, and she never remarried. Grandma protected Dad and rescued him from financial irresponsibility and any consequences from his alcoholism or infidelity. This relationship was part of an unspoken secret that everyone knew but avoided talking about. Later I understood that families are as sick as their secrets.

When I was six, we moved to our own home two blocks from Grandma's house.

Mom worked nights on the pediatric unit at St. Luke's Hospital. Looking forward to Mom tucking us in before leaving was special. I could smell the Estee cologne she wore as she leaned down to kiss me. Dressed in her white nurse's uniform with the round registered nurse pin on the side and her starched nurse's cap ready to work made me so proud of her. I hugged her and said "good night" as she turned off my bedroom light.

Wide-eyed with excitement, Greg and I asked Mom one day to explain to us the grisly details about the sickest person she ever saw. "Well, while training in surgery, I carried an amputated leg to the hospital basement." Mouths wide open and in astonishment, we asked, "What did the leg look like? Was it heavy, and were you afraid of it? Was it a man's leg?" With a gleam in my eyes, I told mom how proud I was that she was a nurse. With my head tilted back and my chest thrust out, I said, "Mom, you're smarter than the rest of the moms in this neighborhood, even in this city! Look how many kids come to you when they're hurt, and their parents know you'll take good care of them. You calm them down when their lips are quivering while blood is running down their leg or arm."

Looking back, I wonder if only someone would have recognized I was suffering during those times, with blood oozing from my heart and soul. Not knowing how to stop it, I acted out my pain and fear in destructive ways. I had a growing sense of shame and betrayal as Dad continued to molest me. Often I wondered if I had acted in a manner that encouraged him to rape me. He would tell me that Mom no longer liked doing what he was to me.

Mom desired to stay home, but Dad's income was unreliable, bringing home what was left after spending evenings at the Blue Moon Bar. Mom kept our heads above water financially and emotionally. She was my life preserver when I was flailing in deep waters, struggling for my next breath. She was my lighthouse when I wandered in darkness, consistently guiding me to safety.

I had another half hour to ride my bike and make it home before the streetlights came on. Riding along the twisted sidewalk at my elementary school was a regular routine. As I slowly rode past an open window, I heard my mother's voice talking to the principal, Mr. Swim. I stopped and listened. "I don't know what has happened to Barbara. She was always a shy, quiet child, but her entire personality began to change about a year ago when she was seven. She's defiant, angry, disobedient, and holds her feelings in. I don't know what else to do. She has even been arrested for calling in false fire alarms. Mr. Ferguson calls me about every other week because Barbara is so disruptive in his class. What is strange is she doesn't seem to be a problem in her other classes. Mrs. Deban or Mrs. Hegwood have never contacted me about her behavior. She gets fairly good grades; I just don't know what to do." I snickered and said to myself, "Good," as I rode off.

I recognized years later how angry and abandoned I felt, lacking the ability to verbalize how I felt. By age eleven a tight corset of rage drove me to malicious acts. Vandalizing cars and property occurred about every week. Calling in false fire alarms got me my first arrest. Tucked away deep in my soul and heart was the sense my home and school were on fire.

One late afternoon restlessness and despondency were so intense I longed to leave the family and the state of Iowa. Not aware of how to find a solution, I dialed the operator and asked if she could help me. Without telling her why I needed assistance, I said, "Can you help me find someone to come and pick me up so I can leave this house?" "Call your parents or relatives or go to a friend's house, and they can help you," she responded. Months later, I was taken to a social worker who advised my parents to not leave me alone, as the therapist believed I was suicidal. The next morning Dad was home, and Mom was at a meeting. He said, "Are you going to bump yourself off or what? I got a lot of work to do." Life was never taken very seriously, so we laughed it away like every other red flag.

A sturdy wall was forming around my heart and mind. Insensitive to the needs of others, I bullied weaker kids at school, drank alcohol, smoked pot, and sniffed glue. I thought I projected an indestructible image and dressed in the armor of a warrior daily.

My brother, Greg, was high maintenance. He was hyperactive and emotional and was my fraternal grandmother's favorite grandchild, so he spent much of his time at her home, two blocks from our house. Greg had nightmares, at which time he would run outside or into my room shouting and crying about things that made no sense. Greg has a disorder we've come to know as trichotillomania, where he pulled out all his eyelashes. At the time, no one knew the name and didn't know of any treatment. Greg was called names by Dad and others who did not attempt to understand or seek help.

In time I realized I come from a line of strong women and weak men. When I was home with Greg and Dad, chaos and agitation caused continuous battles. By the age of fourteen, I suffered with panic attacks and digestive problems resulting in increased drug use.

Dad ran off with other women and would disappear for days, and I found myself jealous, resenting him for being with another woman. Layered on top of my resentment was an intense disgrace for feeling jealous. I knew Mom was alone and weary, working to keep all the plates spinning. One day I saw her touching her temples while closing her eyes and making a deep and noisy sigh. I only made the problems more complicated with my behavior and illnesses. Her call to be a wife and mother was not an easy journey.

Moses, a major spiritual leader in the Old Testament, was worn out from leading the Jewish people out of Egypt. God used Moses to free the Jews from slavery in Egypt. Moses compares his burden to care for the people to a woman bearing, nursing, and attending to the needs of babies. He was overwhelmed by the responsibilities of so many people who acted like wayward children. Indignant at such expectations from the Lord, he questions God, hoping to deter Him. In Numbers 11:11–13 (NIV), Moses refuses to accept his leadership role and suggests that this is God's responsibility. He asks the Lord:

> Why have you brought this trouble on your servant? What have I done to displease you that you put the burden of all these people on me? Did I conceive all these

people? Did I give them birth? Why do you tell me to carry them in my arms, as a nurse carries an infant, to the land you promised on oath to their ancestors? Where can I get meat for all these people? They keep wailing to me.

Old Testament prophets and poets used images of God taken from the realm of a strong and noble female keeping silent in pain.

Isaiah 42:14 (NIV), "For a long time I have kept silent, I have been quiet and held myself back. But now, like a woman in childbirth, I cry out, I gasp and pant."

God is described as performing tasks and roles that are often culturally determined as female.

In Psalm 22:9–10 (NIV), God is portrayed as a midwife who pulls a baby from the womb and places it on its mother's breast.

"Yet you brought me out of the womb; you made me trust in you, even at my mother's breast. From birth I was cast on you; from my mother's womb you have been my God."

In one translation God cuts the umbilical cord in Psalm 71:6 (CEB):

"I've depended on you from birth—you cut the cord when I came from my mother's womb. My praise is always about you."

In Hosea 11:3–4 God self-identifies as a parent who teaches a child, picks up a baby to nuzzle it, and bends down to feed it.

Some Bible scholars believe one of the definitions of the Hebrew word *Shaddai* in Hebrew is the word for breasts. Many translate El Shaddai as the Almighty. God the Almighty also can mean "the multi-breasted God." All body parts that come in pairs (or more than two) are feminine nouns except for a pair of breasts, which is a masculine noun. The idea of God being portrayed by teats doesn't sit well in our Western culture.

Isaiah 66:13 (NIV): God as a comforting mother God, "As a mother comforts her child, so I will comfort you; you shall be comforted in Jerusalem." Isaiah 49:15 (NIV): God compared to a nursing mother, "Can a mother forget the baby at her breast and have no compassion on the child she has borne? Though she may forget, I will not forget you!"

Understanding God with female images comforts and acknowledges the nurturing characteristic of God. Women are not second to men but of equal value and importance. I could not comprehend why I endured such shame when I had a strong and caring mother.

Mom's fractured marriage and in-laws who remained in denial helped compel her to become the leader in the family. She endured the betrayal by her husband and showed determination to create a home for her children. Alone most of the time, she acquired the tenacity to stand for truth and not cower or be intimated by her in-laws.

Dad's mother and sister made a weak man of him, never allowing him to experience the consequences of his behaviors. I recollect watching Dad's mom chase him down the street as he hid in one of his lady friend's basements. I observed women in the family who had to endure challenges that ultimately made them stronger. Disillusioned and disappointed, Mom did not allow the embarrassment she felt at a failed marriage to deter her from her responsibilities.

"I'll only be in the hospital a couple of days," I heard Mom say. She was going to enter St. Luke's Hospital for a biopsy on her right breast. She would spend two nights, but if cancer was found, it could be weeks.

Walking home from seventh grade at McKinley Junior High, I walked by St. Luke's on the way home the day Mom entered. I stopped across the street and looked up at the fourth floor, hoping I might see Mom at the window. The snow was starting to look like a landscape frosted with sweet whiteness. The wet snow soaked through my thin boots and thick socks. *What are Greg and I going to do if she has cancer and dies?* The possibilities terrified me.

Children under fourteen were not allowed on the floors to visit patients. That night around dinner time, I slipped out of the house and went to the hospital. I sat in the general entrance waiting room. Gradually I walked toward the elevators and pushed the button for the fourth floor. Looking in both directions, I started walking down the hallway looking for her room, number 407. I heard my aunt tell family members her room number. A small waiting area and conference room were conveniently across the hall. I opened the heavy door to the waiting area and stood behind it, hoping no one would notice me. I watched outside the small window on the door and could see Mom in a chair in her room knitting. Though I couldn't see Dad, he was talking. His words are indelible in my mind. "If they cut off your breasts, what do you expect me to do? I don't know if I can stay married." My body filled with adrenalin and rage as I watched Mom continue to knit, never looking up. The tests were negative, and soon Mom was home. I never told her what I heard, but I never forgot.

As the years passed, Mom courageously objected to her mother-in-law and sister-in-law, who continually rescued Dad from unwise financial decisions and behaviors. Mom quit covering up for Dad's absence at family events and excusing him for broken promises. I witnessed Dad's mom and my mother, two strong, hurting women, go head to head like verbal wrestlers trying to be nice to one another but win the match. It was educational and fascinating to observe the battle for the family while denying the minefields everyone tried to avoid. Efforts at marriage counseling worked momentarily, but it was like trying to stop a punctured artery with a thin bandage. Mom had Dad committed to a psychiatric unit a couple of times due to his bizarre talk and behavior, but to his demise, he was able to talk his way to freedom.

Mother was creative and thoughtful; she made cards and placed them in our lunch pails as well as placed cards at the table during holidays. She wrote several articles in response to newspaper editorials that presented only one side of an issue or disputed opinions with facts.

Mom developed relationships with women she worked with, and I'm sure she confided in one or two about her marriage and concern for Greg and me. We had no voice or choice, and Mom was our advocate. Though she didn't divorce Dad until years later, I watched her take daring steps toward declaring the truth about him. She spoke to break the painful silence that aided the dysfunction and confusion.

Like most female teenagers, I was obsessed with my appearance, particularly my weight and body.

"Why aren't you eating, Barbara?"

"I'm not hungry, Mom."

"But you're getting too thin, and I'm worried about you."

One of my efforts to control my life that was so out of control was not to eat or to binge on cheap cheeseburgers, fries, and milkshakes, then stick my finger down my throat and purge or take laxatives. Downing laxatives by the handfuls helped guarantee the extraction of unwanted food. One night as my thin body was stretched on the couch, Mom knelt down by me and said that if I didn't eat, she would not eat either.

"I love you, and you're my child, and I want to feel your pain."

I panicked. "No, Mom, don't do it; you're a good nurse, fabulous mom, and human being." That night I opened the medicine cabinet in the bathroom and took out the half bottle of valium; it was about twenty-five pills. Flipping open the pop top on a Budweiser light beer, I downed about six pills, then three more. I don't remember stopping, but I woke up with a tube down my nose and a pan of vomit next to an emergency room bed. A doctor leaned over the bed, asking:

"Why...why did you do this?" Looking away, I shrugged my shoulders.

I was admitted, and the next day the pastor of the Palm Valley Presbyterian Church, Dr. Arnold, walked in my room with a smile and sat down.

"Hi, Barbara. I'm Dr. Arnold from Palm Valley Church. Your mom attends our church, and she called me last night and asked if I'd come to talk to you. Do you mind?"

Feeling as though my brain was leaking through my ears, I smiled and nodded yes. My mind felt like a dismal whitish fog, but I turned to listen in a semi-respectful manner. Halfway through his visit, I still had no idea why he was there or what he was saying. He just talked, never asking a question.

Finally he said, "Can we pray?" Nodding yes again, he began a rather lengthy and masterful prayer. With the "amen" he stood and patted my hand and left.

Shortly after I was discharged, I returned to New York. Unfortunately, I had to take myself with me. Under the illusion things would be different, I made flight reservations the next day for LaGuardia Airport. Mom's eyes were pained with a watery gaze from her tears. She was my hero, and I couldn't continue to bring her suffering. I realize Mom worried just as much when I was away, but at least she had the comfort and faith that God could still rescue me. Mom sent cards to me in New York weekly. I was convinced I failed miserably at being a daughter, but her encouragement and love felt like my soul was being nurtured by a cascade of unending snow cones in a stifling desert.

"Package for you downstairs," my neighbor said on the intercom in my apartment complex. "Want me to bring it up?"

"That would be great," I said.

It was wrapped in brown paper, and I knew it was a book from Mom. Tearing off the paper, I saw a yellow and brown book cover

51

with a design in the center and the title *The Living Bible*. Somewhat disappointed, I threw it on my bed and lay down beside it. Inside the first page, Mom wrote, "To my wonderful daughter, may you find hope and new life in these words." It was followed by a scripture from some book in the Bible called 2 Corinthians, chapter 5:14–21 (NIV):

> For Christ's love compels us, because we are convinced that one died for all, and therefore all died. And he died for all, that those who live should no longer live for themselves but for...Therefore, if anyone is in Christ, the new creation has come: The old has gone, the new is here! All this is from God, who reconciled us to himself through Christ and gave us the ministry of reconciliation: that God was reconciling the world to himself in Christ, not counting people's sins against them. And he has committed to us the message of reconciliation. We are therefore Christ's ambassadors, as though God were making his appeal through us. We implore you on Christ's behalf: Be reconciled to God. God made him who had no sin to be sin for us, so that in him we might become the righteousness of God.

Thumbing through the Bible, I noticed Mom had highlighted scriptures she believed were important for me to read. What care and love only a mother could generate even when her child lived in a perpetual self-destructive and selfish life. I was drawn to the words in the twenty-first verse of 2 Corinthians 5 (NIV); it states, "God made him [Jesus] who had no sin to be sin for us, so that in him we might become the righteousness of God." This statement reverberated in my mind and heart. It wasn't until after I became a Christian that I understood the magnitude of what the verse meant. The Christ, who was sinless, took our filthy, contaminated, impure spiritual condition and put it on Himself and took His pure, holy, and sinless spiritual status and gave it to us. This is why He had to go to the cross; He carried our sin and depraved condition, paying the torturous price of His life so we can be clean before God by His imputed righteousness. Words cannot describe how eternally grateful I am that my mom sent me the Bible. She believed and cherished the knowledge that it was living and active and the only thing that would bring me hope. Occasionally the ultimate perfect gift is given to a person who tosses that present aside. One day the person brings out the gift and is in a stage of life that makes that prize the most valuable and treasured item he or she has ever received. It is a matter of timing, and sometimes the gift is not esteemed until it is hopelessly needed. That's how it was with the Bible Mom sent me that I conveniently hid until the time when the living words became the foundation for my life. Mom stuck by me in the most difficult times, including when I made several trips to Florida, attempting to regroup and pull my life together. Though nothing changed within me, when I felt ready, I returned to New York City. It was like being in a boxing ring with the heavyweight champion of the universe, only it was evil forces in the spiritual realm, and I could on no occasion ever win. Dragging myself out of the ring each time, I shamefully returned to Florida in a cycle of insanity that only the power of a benevolent God could conquer.

Keeping music on, working, attending parties, and endless alcohol and drugs temporarily kept me immune to powerful emotions and my dangerous lifestyle. My brain was trained from childhood to be hypervigilant, always pumping adrenaline to live in the drama and chaos. I recreated my family and was drawn to the "bad boys" like the mafia with charismatic personalities. Even though I was assured I would be cared for and rewarded for sleeping with these racketeers, it was too heavy a price that contributed to contemplating suicide as an option out of pain. My rewards ranged from clothing, money, vacations, or good old hard cash. Dating mobsters appealed to my need to feel safe but provided the opposite.

Continuing to contend with my addictions, I checked into a detox facility every eight to ten months but ignored following through with twelve-step groups and sponsorship. I rationalized that the program worked for them, but it wouldn't work for me. Fresh out of detox, I determined that being intentional every day and utilizing self-control and discipline was enough to keep me clean and sober. If I had been brutally honest with myself and others trying to help me, I would have acknowledged that I could not recall when and if I had ever had self-control or was intentional about quitting. Most people know that it is the definition of insanity to continue to do the same thing over and over expecting a different result. After a week of remorse, I bargained with my deceived, easily rationalized self to just drink on weekends. My method and ways never worked, and the walls I built around my heart and soul became thicker as a means to not feel the shame and disappointment. My heart was one of stone that developed indifference and insensitivity to the needs of others. A broken heart can become a frozen heart, resulting in a darkened perception of others, making it easier to scam them. A hardened heart is padded with open lacerations and deep fractures that are covered with coats of denial and lies.

Insight: What defenses cover your deep heart aches? What has helped you heal your wounds and learn to love again?

Chapter 5:

Oh, What a Tangled Web We Weave
When First We Practice to Deceive

"What's wrong with little white lies?" I asked my teacher, who had caught me in a lie. "Ask your parents," she replied. Of course, I never asked because Dad modeled consistent lying when it suited him.

Dad pulled into the gravel parking lot of the Hideaway Bar. "Don't tell your mom I brought you here," Dad whispered to me as he slipped two dollars in my coat pocket. "Come in with me, and I'll buy you a Coke." The harsh winter wind had blown large snow drifts on the sidewalk, so Dad picked me up from school that day. I stomped the excess snow from my boots and followed him. I squinted to adjust to the dark room of loud voices and a jukebox playing Bobby Darin singing "Mack the Knife." Sitting at the bar with Dad, he introduced me to the bartender, who immediately put a Coke in front of me. I saw a sign that said, "Welcome to happy hour," but I didn't witness happy expressions, only superficial conversations with some slurring speech. Laughter turned to tears after a few shots of whiskey or vodka. While finishing the fifth Coke, I told Dad we needed to go home. Even when he said yes, I knew it would be another half hour or longer. Finally, we made our way to the door. As my eyes adjusted to the light, I questioned why the inside of a bar was so dark.

Years later I recalled the countless times Dad bribed me with money to lie to Mom about where he took me while under his care.

As he sat at the piano with his bourbon next to him, Dad pounded out and sang Dean Martin's famous "Everybody Loves Somebody." Oblivious to anyone around him, Dad never appeared to consider anyone but himself. Eventually we drove home. "Tell your mother you were at Linda's house if she asks." Dad not only initiated lies with ease but acclaimed his skill to deceive others without confrontation or consequences. He educated me; he was my model that said lying promised freedom from punishment and the potential consequences of the actions lied about. There was no thought of the injury to others or damage done to a person's soul and mind. After years of believing he could sustain a life of lies and fantasies, few people trusted anything he said. Toward the end of his life, Dad was unable to decipher fantasies from the truth. Brain damage from years of drinking and fighting became increasingly evident. When children are taught that lying is an effective way to dodge responsibility or consequences, relationships and careers are destroyed. People who color lies or categorize them as big and little lies allow them to justify the deceit. Many say, "It was only a white lie," but lies don't come in colors. "Just tell them I'm not here" is a common lie we ask others to say in our behalf. Dishonesty alienates people and masks a false sense of being in control. The damage and consequences of a life of deception are unrelenting and produce a lifetime of harm. Falsehoods fragment families and communities by eroding trust, and the result is isolation.

One afternoon riding home with Dad, he said he had lost his sunglasses the night before. "Here's how you get sunglasses, Barb."

He pulled into the parking lot of one of the best steakhouses in town and stopped. "I'm going in and will tell the person who greets me that I left my sunglasses here the other night. When they bring the box, just take the pair you like; I'm sure they won't miss them. Most of the glasses have probably been there in lost and found for months.

Chronic liars can have a narcissistic personality disorder. Narcissists have an inflated sense of their own importance, a desire for boundless attention and admiration, troubled relationships, and a lack of empathy for others. Their inability or resistance to recognize the needs and feelings of others results in expecting special treatment while feeling superior to others. They can lie without breaking a sweat. Narcissists are good manipulators that don't share the same worldview as most people. They feel no guilt or shame when they cause someone to feel unhappy or wounded. Selfish and self-centered, they only give attention and priority to their own goals and desires. Attempts to overpower a narcissist usually result in retaliation to gain back the control they feel they are losing. Unable to receive criticism from others, they can become angry and impatient when not receiving their own way. Resorting to violence can occur when someone who is narcissistic feels out of control. The mind and heart are able to justify theft with irrational and immature thoughts in people like my father. Hopefully he knew in some region of his heart and soul he was stealing.

Little doubt my father was a skilled narcissist with a charismatic personality, a talented musician on the piano, and a handsome man. Convincing and hard to resist, he usually triumphed over adversity and regularly got his own way. If I was in a grocery store with Dad and there was a long line (usually women), Dad would say, "Excuse me, ladies, I have to catch a plane and ask if I could go ahead of you." Smiling, those in line cheerfully said, "Oh sure, go ahead." He was a creative and a culinary artist. Several times in the store with him, he would be selecting a certain tasting sauce. As we strolled down the aisles, Dad would take the lid of sauces, dip his finger in the sauce, and taste it. Either it was "perfect," or he replaced the lid and put it back on the shelf.

Only truth-telling creates intimacy, security, and trust. The power of social media has constructed its own sovereign platform for spreading lies and deception. People practice self-deception when they declare their beliefs without regard for truth. Emotions can easily favor facts in order to persuade others to accept what we say. People may not intentionally lie but avoid thoroughly checking out the authenticity of claims because we want our claim to be true. Protecting an image of how we want others to see us is also a common reason for posting half-truths or blatant deception on social media.

Talking with someone in person can develop a healthier and more interdependent relationship. Body language, voice tone, and eye contact contribute to healthy communication and relationships. Pretending to be who we are not is more challenging in person-to-person dialogue.

There was a man in the Old Testament named Abraham. He was a man of great faith and favor with God. Two times Abraham lied about his wife, Sarah, when he entered a foreign land because he feared losing his life. Sarah was supremely beautiful, and he feared that the Pharaoh would kill him. Though great faith defined much of Abraham's life, he still had moments of weakness, and one of his vulnerabilities was lying to avoid conflict. Lying was passed down to his son Isaac and his wife, Rebekah, with severe consequences to his grandchildren. Deception fragmented the family and separated twin boys. To deceive someone means you take from them items they are willing to give you based on the false belief they are helping you (Genesis 12:10–20). The first time he lied was in Genesis 12. Abraham feared the Egyptians would kill him because they would desire to take Sarah for their own. The second time Abraham lied because of fear (Genesis 20:2–7), he told a half-truth and not only led Sarah into sin, but King Abimelek took action based on Abraham's lie of omission.

Abraham's son Isaac and his wife, Rebekah, experienced the crumbling of their family due to deceit. They had twin boys, Jacob and Esau, who became rivals because of the conspiracy Rebekah planned to deceive her husband regarding the birthright. Rebekah favored Jacob, who was the secondborn, and she did not want the slightly older Esau to have his father's birthright and blessing reserved for the firstborn. The practice of deceit continued to affect the lives of this family for years. Though a painful reconciliation occurred, years were wasted, and wounds were deep because of the deception practiced in the family. Exaggeration and half-truths are part of lying and are easier to excuse. But in a court of law in America, we still put one hand on the Bible and promise to tell the truth, the whole truth, and nothing but the truth, so help us, God.

Ready to excel in my career as a travel agent, I was offered a position with a better salary and location. Tour Allure Travel was opening in a newly constructed mall in the heart of Pompano Beach. After six months, I was promoted to assistant manager.

"Hi, I'm Steven; you must be new here." Writing an airline ticket, I dropped my pen and looked up. In front of me was a tall, captivating man with dark curly hair and a charming smile. Steven owned and operated a stereo store in the mall with the latest technology in audio sound. We spent time together, and our relationship grew into a mutual love. Steven was Jewish, so I learned to make some rather delicious matzo ball soup and educated myself on Jewish family traditions. The value of family and tradition in most Jewish homes was appealing. His family appeared to approve of me, which felt as though I had overcome a huge hurdle in order to move forward. When I was with Steven, I ignored the distractions and believed we could get married. In the tenth month of dating, I moved into Steven's one-bedroom apartment near the mall. His business was flourishing, and I was delighted to go to his store during my lunch break and bring him coffee. Finally happiness no longer eluded me. Though Steven had his issues, I loved him and felt a sense of normalcy in our life together. I trusted Steven and had no reason not to believe him. Some months later, Steven stopped coming by the travel agency during his breaks. Not wanting to smother him, I didn't say anything. A contemporary retail dress store operated across from where I worked. Steven began spending time with a salesperson named Laura. Realizing I could see them together, he told me before I asked, "Laura's parents and mine are friends, and she just got the job at Young Sophisticates clothing store. They asked me to check on her and protect her like a sister." He reached over the table while we were having dinner and kissed me. "Don't worry; I love you, and nothing is going on."

On birth control for over a year, I was in disbelief when I discovered I was pregnant. Not knowing antibiotics can, on occasion, overrule birth control pills, I was in a daze for days. What would Steven say? I was sure he'd want us to marry. His words will forever be engrained in my mind. "I'm not ready to be a dad. I think you should move back home with your mom till we work this out." As I began to cry, one hand covered my mouth, and the other held me up as I grabbed onto the door. Barely able to drive home, I was thankful when I pulled in the driveway. Running up the stairs, I opened the door and fell on my bed. Mom came in the room, and I told her. As she was holding me, we cried together. I continually called Steven that night and for the next three days with no answer. I sat near the phone those days, despondent at times, trying to accept that Steven had deserted me.

The following week Steven came to see me and informed me that he had to think about what to do and that he'd call me in a few days. I instinctively knew he was with Laura. He ran out of our house into his green Corvette and drove off, afraid my brother would beat the crap out of him. Decisions needed to be made about this child in my womb. I wanted to marry Steven and have the baby. Abortions had just been legalized in New York State, and Steven wanted me to have an abortion. My mind and heart were weighted down as I considered the options. My mind felt like an overloaded electrical system ready to blow a fuse.

Steven had made arrangements before I actually made the decision. I would stay with his parent's friends, Harold and Muriel Berkman, who lived in Far Rockaway, Long Island. Two days later, I was taking off from Fort Lauderdale Airport en route to LaGuardia. I sat next to a woman who appeared sad and revealed she was going to New York to bury her brother, who had died suddenly. I told myself I was going to New York to kill my baby and bury him or her.

Muriel and Harold embraced me with open arms. They made conversation uncomplicated and effortless. We discussed how Steven and I met and details of the relationship. That evening I had an appointment with the doctor who would perform the abortion. The Beekmans remained positive for my sake and provided all the comforts of home. Every detail was discretely prepared without challenges. Though disguised by professionalism and great amenities, the sting of having an abortion and killing a life would have long-lasting effects. The next afternoon I was admitted to the hospital, and the procedure was scheduled for the following morning. That night I lay awake battling the decision to abort this baby and what would happen when I returned to Florida. Steven called that night and said he had surprises for me when I returned home. Perhaps he wanted me to live with him again or get married, but his commitment and love for me were fading quickly. As I was wheeled into the surgical room, my heart pounded like the loud bass of a song.

A painful and shaming moment came in the recovery room when a nurse said to me in a detestable and dismissive tone of voice, "It was a boy." The recent legalization of abortion in the state of New York remained a controversial law—I'm sure. Though I believe the nurse was wrong in saying what she did, I understand now how difficult it is for pro-life believers. If I had taken the time and effort to investigate when life began and the process of abortion, I may have made a different decision. The abortion was constantly in my mind, especially when I witnessed women with newborn babies. Living with unrelieved regret was toxic, and it was not until I found forgiveness in Jesus Christ, who paid the price for all sins, that I was fully forgiven. It was a process of acceptance and letting go.

I am opposed to abortion and believe all life, including babies who die before birth, is with the Lord and we will see them someday. One of the most meaningful and beautiful Psalms for me is Psalm 139. If a person needs assurance that God is not distant and that He knows that person completely, this is one of the best portions of Scripture to share. It is also a strong word that contradicts abortion. In the New Living Translation of the Bible, Psalm 139:13–16 says:

> You made all the delicate, inner parts of my body and knit me together in my mother's womb. Thank you for making me so wonderfully complex! Your workmanship is marvelous—how well I know it. You watched me as I was being formed in utter seclusion, as I was woven together in the dark of the womb. You saw me before I was born. Every day of my life was recorded in your book. Every moment was laid out before a single day had passed.

Abortion is not an "unforgivable sin." There are many factors that go into a woman's decision to abort a life. Options for placement and adoption are numerous in our culture today. The church has been part of providing a variety of choices for women who are contemplating abortion.

In our current culture, multifunctional homes and facilities are available for expectant mothers who can remain until after the baby is born. Some services allow for mother and baby to remain in the program for up to a year or more. Newer accommodations are suited for expectant moms to bring other children while waiting for the new life to be birthed. Abortion is acceptable to many in the culture because of an emphasis on a woman's rights and the fragmentation of the family system. Individualism and entitlement issues are a strong voice in the liberal and feminist philosophy. The focus is on a woman's right to control her own body while silencing the fetus, who has a heartbeat as early as three weeks. My decision was the ultimate rejection of personal responsibility and selfishness. In my case I allowed fear and believed I would be a horrible mother to guide the choice. It was self-centered; it was the easy way out. I'm not condemning myself, but I am merely facing my truth. Comforting and not condemning anyone for aborting a baby is my purpose. Guilt and shame can weigh heavy for years. Friends said to me, "Barb, it's not fair to bring a child into the life you are living. Look at your track record and who would take care of the child...Steven and his girlfriend?" It was not the ideal circumstance to raise a child, but I've witnessed young ladies who have gotten their life together when they became a mother.

Steven and I talked a couple of times when I returned. Being in the electronic business, he brought me a portable television, earphones, music tapes, and more. I'm sure it was a guilt offering. I understand why he did that, but it wasn't material "stuff" I needed. I mourned for months as Steven slowly left the shore of my life like a sailboat in the horizon. He married Laura, and they had a number of children. Steven died a few years after their last child was born of an apparent heart attack.

Sadly, there will be millions of unborn children in heaven who were not allowed to be born due to abortion. It's obvious that among those who were destroyed before they met the world existed possible future scientists, musicians, and leaders who could have left their unique fingerprints for making the world a better place.

Insight: Are you or someone you know living with the shame of having an abortion? Reach out the Christ, and you will find forgiveness and unconditional love.

I picked up the phone uncertain of the time, but I knew it was after midnight.

"Were you sleeping?" Jackie asked.

"Yes, I was, but what's up?"

"Sorry to call so late. I forgot you're on Pacific Time."

"Jackie, you continue to forget and phone me before 11:00 p.m. your time."

The next morning, I questioned Jackie's recurrent late-night and early-morning calls. Why couldn't she call me at a decent hour? Later that day I remembered that Jackie, like me, had no privacy or boundaries as a child growing up in St. Louis. Calling to mind her story, she told me of living in a dysfunctional family that didn't practice respect for one another or honor the word "no." As a new Christian, Jackie did not understand the importance of respecting the boundaries of others, which meant being considerate of their time, space, and resources.

I was unaware of a right to privacy or knocking before entering a room—it was foreign to me because I had no boundaries as a child. As Dr. Henry Cloud and Dr. John Townsend say in their 1992 bestselling book *Boundaries*, "In the physical world, boundaries are easy to see. Fences, signs, walls, rivers with alligators, and manicured lawns or hedges are all boundaries. They mark a visible property line that someone owns."[iii] Boundaries are anything that helps to differentiate us from someone else. One of the first God-given boundaries all humans are given is the gift of skin. Skin keeps our insides protected and in place. A boundary shows us where we begin and end. One of the first realizations of boundaries is when an infant begins to understand that he or she is not an extension of mommy and that the child and mom are separate people. Boundaries take several forms, such as physical, emotional, and the right to agree or disagree. When the option to decline another person's physical or emotional advances is ignored, a gross injustice occurs.

When a child is overpowered by someone stronger who is physically, sexually, or verbally abusive, the ultimate boundary line is destroyed and becomes invisible. A lack of boundaries for a child who has been abused makes it challenging as an adult to respect anyone who has strong boundaries.

Insight: When boundaries are not allowed in our homes when we are children, we can fail to know how to set boundaries as adults. Are you good with setting boundaries? For a young child victimized by another's brutalizing touch, more than just his or her flesh is violated.

The root of all that constitutes a human being is attacked and desecrated when all boundaries are violated by abuse. Innocence is ripped from the soul, and the sacredness of the body is burglarized and pillaged. It is an invasion of a person by an enemy who often masquerades as a caring friend or family member. Routine, peaceful living, and honoring others' limits were foreign to me. Rarely refusing a date with a man for fear of rejection complicated my life, especially when I knew there would probably not be a second date.

At age seventeen, I dated a man in New York while living in an apartment paid for by another man associated with organized crime. The man associated with the criminal syndicate was tender and made sure I had whatever I needed. I yearned for security with a person of power who could take whatever action necessary to nurture and support me.

At eighteen I described myself as a free person and able to make my own life choices. No rules or restrictions could limit my behavior as I sought to fulfill my desires. Lacking self-discipline and not an ounce of wisdom, I became a slave to my appetites and pleasures.

Still living with Mom, I knew I needed to respect her and share in the duties of cooking and cleaning. This included coming home at a decent hour and locking up before retiring for the night.

The delusion that a new beginning in a different location could stop the self-destructive behavior is completely absurd. Feelings of worthlessness, failure, and fear heightened the panic attacks. Terror of death plagued me and was only temporally muzzled by alcohol or drugs.

Managing a travel agency in Midtown Manhattan on Madison Avenue would perhaps impress some people; the address alone made a flashy impression. But dressing up my outward image did not change my internal reality of a shame-based identity. Laboring endlessly to impact others demanded increasing energy. Engaging in superficial, inauthentic conversations always camouflaged my frightful hidden loneliness.

Alphonse, my married boyfriend, invited me to attend President Nixon's inaugural ball in DC. Preparing for the event was more glamorous and fun than the actual affair. Beauty salon, shopping for the ideal dress, and lavish restaurants were a splendid hors d'oeuvre to the influential big evening. We arrived at the Kennedy Center, where I expected to be served an elegant dinner. To my surprise I was handed a plastic cup with weak sparkly punch. Hoping I'd make a lasting impression, I danced with several senators, congressmen, and governors. Champagne and an assortment of alcoholic beverages flowed while the level of loud intoxicated voices made it difficult to hear the speakers.

The first six months in New York were exciting, but soon I began to look for an apartment. Grabbing a free apartment resource guide as I left the market, I started looking. "Yes, this might be an option."

I circled an ad for a room to rent in a condo on First Avenue and Twenty-second Street. I made an appointment to see the room, and a young college student answered, "Hi, I'm Carla," as she stuck her hand out to welcome me. Carla was living in the two-bedroom condo alone and attending college nearby. Her mother had died a couple of years earlier, and her father was living in Africa.

Carla was a mature seventeen-year-old and graciously allowed me to rent a room. While I was taking the last box to my room, the fragrance of olive oil and garlic sizzling in a pan caused me to smile. "I'm making eggplant parmesan; would you like to stay for dinner?" Carla blurted from the kitchen. With her long black hair and big brown eyes, she reminded me of a scene from *The Godfather*. She was a true Italian beauty. Always taking a gift when invited to dinner, I gratefully declined. Feeling like a phony, I determined Carla would not see me intoxicated.

I'm going to call on this one, I thought. In the employment section of the paper was an ad for a person to manage a new travel agency on the Upper East Side of Manhattan. I could take the First Avenue bus up to Sixty-first Street and walk a block to work. After a brief conversation, I met one of the owner's staff the next morning. The young man I met was from Iran, and the agency was located in a block of businesses owned predominantly by Persian businessmen. The owner of the travel agency, Mr. Hushang Lavi, was a representative of the Shaw of Iran to purchase Tomcat fighter jets for Iran from Grumman aircraft on Long Island, New York. I thought it peculiar to name a travel agency Tomcat Travel until I understood Mr. Lavi's position in acting for the Shaw and the nation of Iran. Mr. Lavi's job purchasing the fighter jets clarified much of the activities that transpired in the office. Backgammon games were played competitively monthly in a crowded private room in the back of the agency. Men speaking Farsi continued to be heard the next morning as I opened the front door to the agency. The stale smell of cigars and cigarettes hung in the front office as I opened the files. The backgammon tournament had continued through the night, and a variety of fluctuating voices was heard with each move. Sighs and disappointment were heard in the voice inflection with every wrong move made, and clapping and loud approvals were shouted when a team or person won. Later I was told up to $100,000 was bet on each team.

Hushang Lavi was the arms dealer for Iran and the Shaw's chosen man for the job. He was a quiet, shy man who always treated me with respect. Airline tickets to and from Iran and surrounding countries were issued weekly to various Persian businessmen and family. Little accountability was required from me so I could have a couple of drinks or take painkillers at lunch and still do my job.

As the episodes of terror and ensuing apocalyptic doom continued, my visits to hospital emergency rooms increased. I was convinced I was going to die and began to hyperventilate while heart palpitations escalated. I was told it was an "anxiety attack" and given additional tranquilizers. No one warned me about mixing alcohol and Librium or Valium, but I learned the dangers of combining alcohol and depressants by waking up in an emergency room at 3 a.m., unable to recall any details of how I got there or what happened.

Not recognizing I had fallen down the rabbit hole, I felt like Alice in Wonderland, who reached the bottom and was either too large to get through the door or too small to grab the key. I was definitely at my own deadly mad tea party.

"I'm sending you to a psychiatrist in Coney Island who specializes in hypnotizing people to stop certain habits. He's had good results with helping others quit smoking cigarettes and drinking alcohol. I'll make an appointment for this Saturday, and here's his information."

I stood up to leave as Dr. Eighler handed me the information. Putting on my heavy coat, I walked down the stairs of the brownstone building where my psychologist had his office. "Can you drive me to Coney Island Saturday?" I asked my boyfriend. As usual, he consented and picked me up early. Climbing the dark concrete stairs, we entered Dr. Woolman's office. We thought we had entered a synagogue or church when opening the waiting room door. Padded pew-like seating was arranged around tables of magazines. It flashed through my mind that perhaps an offering would be taken in place of a bill. I looked up as a person who was dressed in a peach blouse with a short strand of pearls and jeans walked to the exit. The individual looked like a man but clearly was dressed on top as a woman. It was 1974, and it was rare to hear the word "transgender" or see a person in public who displayed such characteristics. I picked up a flyer on a table that described Dr. Woolman's credentials. He was listed as a psychiatrist, a gynecologist, and a rabbi with various educational institutions and years of graduation. Before I completed reading, a tall, slightly overweight man in a white jacket extended his hand to me and said, "Hello, I'm Dr. Wollman." I followed him to an exam office and sat on the papered exam table. He began explaining the process for sex change surgery and presented me with pictures of men's genitalia and how he built the penis.

"I don't want a sex change!" I blurted out. "Dr. Eichler sent me here to be hypnotized for my smoking and alcohol addiction."

"Oh, I'm so sorry. Follow me." He escorted me into another room that was dimly lit and had a recliner chair. Setting me in the recliner, he turned on a light with an orange glow and a clicking sound as he attempted to hypnotize me. In a soothing, monotone voice, he said, "When I say your initials, you will no longer want to drink alcohol or smoke cigarettes." I heard what he said, but too bewildered to relax or respond, I jumped out of the chair and ran out of the office. My boyfriend followed me and unlocked his car.

"What is wrong, Barbara?" I told him what had happened, and he laughed uncontrollably. "Let's stop at Joe's grill; I need a drink!"

Sifting out men who appeared financially successful and were old enough to be my father was my preference in men. Pursuing a man who would care for me like a good father would motivate my dating behavior. Some of the men were married, which I attempted to forget. I was recreating my family of origin while trying to craft a different outcome. Regardless of the countless times I sought to construct a positive, happy result, it only added to my disgrace and hopelessness.

Repeating the sexual relationship with my father and keeping the secret from my mom was the identical scene I played out with a married man. Showering me with continual drugs, alcohol, and luxurious gifts made it possible for me to give men what they wanted. Though chemicals and gifts brought temporary comfort, the euphoric feelings wore off, and a serious case of self-contempt and criticism moved in.

Genuine freedom is not found in living by my impulses, appetites, and feelings. Feelings are indicators, not dictators. Developing a:

> Personal rule of Life is not about rules as much as a set of guidelines that support or enable us to do the things we need and want to do. It allows us to clarify our deepest values, most important relationships, and to actualize our hopes and dreams. The word "rule" derives from a Latin word, *regula,* which implies a say of regulating or regularizing our lives so we can remain on the path we have set out for ourselves. A rule of life is descriptive because it articulates our intentions and identifies the ways in which we want to live. A rule is like a trellis which offers support and guidance for a plant, helping it to grow correctly. "Your personal rule of life is discerned and framed through the longings, yearnings and goals God has placed on your heart and mind that propel you forward with joy."

A personal rule of lie is formed and reflected in your daily, weekly, monthly, quarterly, and annual relational priorities.

Months slipped away, and the rotating door to detox and treatment continued. If I had insurance, the facilities were not bad, and breakfast was more than watered-down oatmeal. Settling into the new upscale hospital, I plopped on the bed taking stock of my surroundings for the next few weeks.

"Hi, my name is Meg."

"I'm Barb. I guess we are bathroom mates."

"Well, it's good to meet you, Barb, and I hope our stay here is beneficial."

I met Meg at Gracie Square Psychiatric Hospital one afternoon in late spring. It would be the beginning of a lifetime friendship. I was being detoxed from a number of pills and being treated for depression. Meg was receiving care for an intense anxiety disorder.

After discharge, Meg and I remained connected, and after being asked to leave my apartment due to my alcohol and drug use, I moved in with Meg and her boyfriend, Brian. Getting up early day, I applied for jobs in travel and as executive personnel head hunter. In the afternoons I accompanied Meg to many of her auditions for soap operas and a variety of commercials. I will never forget realizing one day that Meg knew I was stealing pain medication and tranquilizers from her medicine cabinet. She removed them and substituted them with vitamins. A kick of fury ran through my stomach and reverberated throughout the rest of my body as I shook my head at how ungrateful and completely self-absorbed I had become. It felt like ice water was running through my veins, and even though I took from Meg, she didn't bring it up or throw me out of her home. She understood the bondage of addiction and self-hate and how substances had imprisoned me and were controlling my life. Sensing another layer of shame being glued to my soul and heart, I let out an uncontrolled moan and waited for Meg to return home. "Meg, how could you still even care about me after stealing from you?" Lowering my gaze to the ground, I let tears fall as Meg put her arms around me and cried with me. A couple of months later, I found a room to rent and moved in. Meg and I remained connected, and I got a job at an executive employment agency on Madison Avenue. I was good at filling job orders because I didn't stop at anything to make some money. I would lie to companies in order to obtain the name of someone in a certain department, and I'd call them if it might be a fit and offer them a better job. Abusing drugs or alcohol or addictive behavior are the symptoms of deeper issues that perpetuate a self-destructive life that ends in death if there is no intervention. Conduct I once bared and would never consider was now permissible. Shooting heroin in a dilapidated building in the Lower East felt like only a nightmare, but it was real, and I found myself there often. After several months of drug use, I woke up in Creedmoor Psychiatric Center in Queens, NY. I'm not sure how I arrived there; another blackout for me to figure out. I was thankful when I knew I had not injured or killed someone in that state of amnesia. I put sixty-five cents in the payphone and called Meg after a couple of days.

"Hi, Meg. I just wanted to let you know in case you were calling me that I'm in Creedmoor State in Queens. I don't remember how I got here, but I'm sure I'll be discharged as soon as I get to speak with a psychiatrist.

"I love you, and don't worry about me, Meg."

"Barbara, Creedmoor is a dangerous place; patients have murdered other patients, and I've heard there is little supervision in the unit. I think I'll come visit you."

"Oh, Meg, you'd have to take a subway here, and it's not worth it. I'll be all right; please don't come. I'll call you when I get to my room."

At that time the state hospitals were only warehouses for the mentally ill with little to no activities. I recall lining up for a shower with no clothes on next to men and women in the same state. If a person had the mental capabilities and a minuscule sense of normalcy and thinking, boredom in that facility made the time go so slowly. I'd become familiar with people who looked and acted as the patients did at Creedmoor, so I wasn't afraid of them. But Meg was afraid for my life.

Two days later, I heard keys jangling as the attendant unlocked the thick, anchored door and opened it for a visitor. My eyes widened as I recognized it was Meg. I ran up to her, hugged her tightly, and asked why she had come.

"Barb, I've seen that guy's face before." She was looking at a patient in the dayroom who I spent a significant amount of time with when he made sense. "He's a murderer, Barb. He murdered three women, and I just can't let you stay here. I have an appointment with the medical director, so I'll come back when I'm done; give me half an hour or so."

I forced a smile as she left and went down the hall. I waited by the door, looking at the wall clock every few minutes. After about forty-five minutes, the door opened, and Meg returned and handed the nurse a form. She walked over to me quickly and grabbed my arm, guiding me to my room.

"You're out of here, Barb, and you're coming with me."

"How is that, Meg? I really haven't even seen a doctor in the past few days."

"Look, they have so many patients here they won't miss you. You see, I put my acting skills to work and told the medical director I was a psychiatrist. Why do you think I'm dressed more business-like? I knew what to say and told him everything he wanted to hear. You are out of here, so pack what you have, and let's go before something happens."

It worked; the hospital released me, and Meg and I walked out together. Being able to walk out of a state hospital as we did was a commentary on the care at this facility. Men and women showered in the same bathroom. Male and female patients stood together in separate lines naked, waiting for the next shower to become available. A staff member stood at the front of the line directing people like cattle waiting to get branded. Groups and activities were nonexistent, and the dayroom was sprinkled with a few tattered books and magazines. Perhaps because the residents were considered seriously mentally ill little effort was made to reach them other than medication and occasional visits by the psychiatrist. The state paid the hospital to warehouse those who were critically mentally ill with little to no effort to improve their daily living skills or mental health. Each of the three state mental hospitals I was placed in due to alcoholic blackouts and anxiety was similar. Two of the hospitals were located in New York, and one in South Florida. The vacant look in the eyes of those who were institutionalized for a significant amount of time was shocking and tragic.

Chapter 6:

Addiction

Because the addiction to chemicals and behaviors becomes completely consuming and demanding, addiction is the most potent form idolatry offers. Truly addiction is a "misguided enactment of our quest for God." The objects of our addiction become our false gods, and we worship them with our energy, time, and love. The addicted settle for immediate gratification through fleeting feelings of euphoria to balance stress and the deep pain of life. But this self-centered life begins to fragment as the state of euphoria turns to misery. Relationships start to splinter; lies and more lies to cover up our disasters cause us to lose a job, and our health declines. A high percentage of the crimes committed by men and women who are incarcerated are drug- and alcohol-related. I recall attending a lecture in which a medical doctor stated that addiction is a disease. I found that difficult to believe, assuming it meant the addict had no control over their actions. But after further education and understanding of the definition given by the lecturer, I accepted why it was categorized as a disease.

In 1956 the American Medical Association (AMA) declared addiction to alcohol and other drugs to be a disease. The American Psychiatric Association (APA) followed the AMA in 1960. Addiction to AOD qualifies as a disease by meeting certain criteria. It became known as the five Ps of addiction because of the following:

1. Primary: It is an illness in its own right, not the result of, complication of, or symptoms of another disease.

2. Predictable: Has a predictable progression that is observable.

3. Progressive: As time passes, the disease always becomes worse.

4. Premature death: Without treatment the addicted person will die.

5. Permanent: Even with treatment the person is subject to the possibility of relapse.

Abusing chemicals is dangerous and destroys everything worthwhile and meaningful to a person. Families are fragmented, and premature death occurs more often than a person realizes. "With the surge and misuse of deadly drugs like fentanyl and other opiates, the death toll has increased significantly since 2014."[iv] Since the COVID pandemic in early 2020, the demand for mental health and substance abuse treatment has soared. Loss of life and complicated grief has added to depression, anxiety, and loneliness throughout the pandemic. Alcohol and drug abuse have multiplied due to isolation, uncertainty, and the loss of jobs and finances. The church has been granted an opportunity to be Christ to the world and to model a loving and welcoming Christian community. Addiction is a prophetic challenge to the church to embrace those who smell of alcohol and urine, but as a pastor reminded me, the stench is why Jesus died.

Some addictions are acceptable in the culture. People replace worshipping the Lord with worshipping of self, children, sports heroes, and music makers. No idol will ever satisfy the profound yearning for God. It has been said by those in twelve-step programs that "we used to drink God out of a bottle." Enough is never enough because addiction is a habit of extremism. An addict or alcoholic will sell their own mother down the river if he or she gets too desperate.

The Daniel Plan: 40 Days to a Healthier Life; *Healthy Gut*; *Before I Eat*; *Healthy Living over Fifty: Live Well and Enjoy Life*; *Love to Eat, Hate to Eat: Breaking the Bondage of Destructive Eating Habits*; *Never Binge Again*; and *Feeding Your Appetite: Take Control of What's Controlling You*. These are just a few book titles I have purchased through the years to gain control over my addiction to sugar and carbohydrates. Understanding the dangers of overeating refined sugar and carbohydrates, I do not stop yielding to these cravings. There have been periods of abstinence from these unhealthy chemicals where I lost weight and felt healthy. Though ten or fifteen pounds overweight, being a borderline diabetic for the past five years has not convinced me to eliminate these unnatural and harmful foods. If I practiced self-control and balance, enjoying a small amount of ice cream, pie, or chips would be sufficient.

One holistic medical doctor told me the culprit is a chemical or malfunction in my brain that is to blame for my inability to stop feeding my appetites and cravings. A craving can become an addiction when a person cannot control his or her response to it. Cravings and habits are common and do not necessarily become addictions. A behavioral or chemical addiction makes it almost impossible to stop oneself from gratifying the desire. Sugar was another escape from stress. Something is activated in me when I think of eating ice cream or other celebratory treats. In the last ten to fifteen years, technology has made it possible to embark on life-altering research and gain knowledge of the brain's structure and function. The brain's own reward system is feeling good and consists of billions of neurons that communicate in the form of electrical impulses. Drugs and alcohol or food tap into the brain's communication system and interferes with the way nerve cells send, receive, and process information. The drugs or chemicals target the brain's reward system by flooding it with dopamine. When the chemicals are removed, the brain reacts with alerting the person to the now unbalanced amount of dopamine. This is part of the withdrawal cycle.

Addiction can be chemical or behavioral. Chemicals taken into the body can range from caffeine to heroin and either stimulate or tranquilize. Behavioral addictions perform the same function of stimulating or sedating. With the rapid advancement of technology, addictions to gambling, shopping, and pornography have increased sharply. If a person has limited accountability, the addiction can remain a secret for longer periods of time. Caffeine, sugar, gluttony, and workaholism remain comparatively acceptable social addictions. Preoccupation with helping others or attending all church events can be utilized to avoid relationships and feelings, and the person is praised and admired for his or her sacrifice and dedication.

The legalization of "THC marijuana in many states has caused increased auto accidents, crime, decreased motivations to study for a range of grades and ages in school, and inability to concentrate in Colorado and California."[v]

Looking in the mirror becomes an exercise in self-deception and denial as we see our idealized self, not the reality of what our addiction has done to us. The unattainable goal of becoming someone other than the person God created causes internal conflict and unrealistic expectations of self and others. Without an eternal perspective, a person expects to experience the level of satisfaction that only eternity can and will provide.

The apartment in New York where I lived was owned by Carla. The illusion that I could control my addictions was shattered. She offered me many chances to keep alcohol, drugs, and men out of the apartment, but since I was unable to fulfill my promises, it was time for me to go. The self-centeredness of chemical abuse disregarded Carla's requests and disrespected her privacy. Her patience and compassion were consumed by my inability to stay sober and the disorganization and disturbance the addiction created in her home.

I was under the influence of narcotics and alcohol continually and stayed with people I met on the street. The rotating door of treatment programs and shelters consumed my energy and left me without options and without hope.

Several years later, sober and a Christian, I located my former roommate Carla's contact information and called her. She was married to a physician and had two boys. As we reminisced about our time together, I began apologizing for the countless times my lifestyle intruded on her life.

"Do you remember the party you took me to in that penthouse on the Upper East Side?" Carla asked. "It's when you worked for the Persian man who owned the travel agency on First Street and Sixty-seventh."

Hurriedly exploring my memory, I carefully answered, "No."

"You insisted we take a cab, Barb, and got to the penthouse about 9:00 p.m. The elevator opened on the penthouse floor, and we walked into two men dressed in well-tailored and expensive navy blue suits. The massive room was void of furniture or décor except for a large fish tank against a wall near the entrance. I was given a drink, took a few sips, and soon realized I'd been drugged. Before passing out I staggered to the bedroom and called Johnnie. Within the hour, he found the building and penthouse and miraculously got me home. For two days I recuperated because I cannot tolerate drugs."

Loaded with guilt and unable to stand, I sat down and said, "Oh, Carla, I am so very sorry. Where was I? Couldn't I help?"

"Barb, you disappeared, and I didn't see you for two weeks. You never said a word about where you were or who you were with."

I felt a sudden jab like a heavy icicle striking my core and felt paralyzed. "I have no memory of that, Carla. I don't even recall taking you to such a party. I know you are telling me the truth, and I cannot apologize enough that I put you in such a dangerous situation."

The conversation ended well, and we even had a laugh at the craziness and chaos I created. After hanging up I fell on my knees and, in tears, began to thank God I was alive and home. A verse in the Old Testament Proverbs describes my impaired lifestyle. It says,

"As a dog returns to its vomit, so fools repeat their folly" (Proverbs 26:11, NIV).

The Bible is filled with warnings against drunkenness. No good ever came from some being drunk. Noah, who built the ark and saved his family, did everything the Lord asked of him, remaining in flood waters for forty days. Noah planted a vineyard and got drunk and lay naked inside his tent. Noah's son Ham disrespected him by not covering his father's naked body, perhaps making fun of him (Genesis 9:20–28). The family was not the same after that incident. After forty days with two of each species of animals and my family, I probably would have planted a vineyard and gotten drunk also! Proverbs 20:1 in The Message says, "Wine makes you mean, beer makes you quarrelsome—a staggering drunk is not much fun."

Proverbs 23:29–35 (NIV) goes into detail about the consequences of alcohol abuse.

> Who has woe? Who has sorrow?
> Who has strife? Who has complaints?
> Who has needless bruises? Who has bloodshot eyes?
> Those who linger over wine,
> who go to sample bowls of mixed wine.
> Do not gaze at wine when it is red,
> when it sparkles in the cup,
> hen it goes down smoothly!
> In the end it bites like a snake and poisons like a viper.
> Your eyes will see strange sights, and your mind will imagine confusing things.
> You will be like one sleeping on the high seas, lying on top of the rigging.
> "They hit me," you will say, "but I'm not hurt! They beat

me, but I don't feel it!
When will I wake up so I can find another drink?"

As I failed to flee my shame and sense of worthlessness, each hour was filled with work or parties. I longed for purpose and to be important to someone who needed me. But I wasn't even important to myself.

In another alcoholic blackout one night, I woke in Bellevue Hospital. Not realizing what I did to get there, I asked a nurse, who told me it was too late and I needed to go to bed. People, young and old, looking like zombies would line up for their morning medications of antipsychotic drugs like Haldol or other sedating drugs. After meds, the white-robed patients sat down to a sterile bowl of oatmeal and plain white bread. Most of the patients appeared to be void of reality or perhaps too drugged to know. Several times I spoke to nurses or attendants on behalf of patients who looked as if they were treated unfairly. It could be my approach and words were threatening, and I became uncooperative and was placed in quiet rooms and hit repeatedly with my own slippers. When I awoke, I realized I'd been given a hypodermic of thioridazine or another strong sedative.

Even after these experiences, I went out as soon as I was released and looked for a job. I interviewed well, and 95 percent of the time was offered the job. A couple of months later, I was waking up in various places and running out of excuses at the job. One night I was told I was tossed on the lawn at Harlem Hospital Center in New York City.

"Hey, you better wake up. What are you doing here?" Leaning over me was a Black woman with a puzzled look talking. As I sat up, I saw I was in a dormitory with of all Black women. I knew it was a hospital and quickly determined I was one of two White women in a detox program for addicts in Harlem Hospital Center in Harlem, New York. A nurse dressed in her white uniform said to me, "We don't take White people, but you were so pathetic we let you stay."

"How did I get here?" I asked.

"Someone had dumped you on the lawn of the hospital, and security brought you here."

I wish they would have told me to go. It was fourteen days of hell. Waking me up at 5 a.m., they told me, "Go clean the bathrooms, you ##!" I remained calm and escaped by daydreaming of a better life. Greens with hotdogs cut up in them and a slice of white bread were served as lunch. It didn't take long to recognize I would not be allowed to leave. I tried escaping one night at 1 a.m. but made it to the elevator, where an elevator operator told me to get back in the room. It was an alcohol and drug treatment program, but there was no program. How could we be kept there without our permission? Where were the group lectures or counseling? We sat in the dormitory all day listening to music.

I didn't dare question the absence of treatment and the lack of explanation of why we were forced to stay there. It was 1975, and civil rights were in the spotlight. Several civil rights laws were signed and enforced by 1975, but in cities like Harlem, New York, racial tensions were escalating. The women in the dorm where I was to spend the next fourteen days could injure me or kill me, and no one would know for a prolonged period of time. Just my presence was dangerous, especially when the women questioned me about my drug and alcohol use, where I lived, and why I was in Harlem Hospital Center, which was reserved for the Black community. Smart enough to keep my mouth shut and do what I was told, I avoided potential harm.

But as I listened to the stories of the women, I understood our needs and desires for a healthy life were not that different. Disappointments and pain drove us to numb all sense of feeling and avoid reality. Since we were unaware of our own potential and putting to death dreams about our life we may have imagined at one time, hope of a better life was minimal or absent. Only the love and power of a kind and merciful heavenly Father could deliver us. Only Jesus Christ could give us fresh dreams and cause us to see ourselves as He sees us. I think of those women and wonder where they are today. I remained in contact with one particular girl, but we did not help one another. We shot heroin together and deadened our senses to our present existence. God is a God of many chances, and it is not how we start but how we finish.

"You got a cigarette?" a thin, muscular woman with a hardened face said to me. Her eyes were vacant and expressionless; she was missing the little finger on her left hand.

"Here, take the pack," I said. She grabbed it and turned around. After five days a couple of women spoke to me about their life and addiction. My listening skills improved as I sat on the flimsy mattress and heard their story.

The woman in charge of the program usually visited every other day. Prancing down the hallway in her designer clothes, she let me know why we were locked down. She only got paid for the ones who stayed. Here was a Black woman using her own community for financial gain. Her nieces and nephews had secured positions as counselors but rarely interacted with the patients. A couple of years later, the program was abolished, and the woman was indicted for fraud against Medi-Cal and state funds. Greed doesn't care about color or gender. Even in the early '70s, this Black woman was scamming her own people who desperately needed hope. On my last evening in Harlem Hospital Center, I cried out to God and promised this time I would clean up my act. I fantasized about what it would be like to have a husband, a decent man, who truly loved me. I wanted to be "good." I just couldn't seem to do it.

When the fourteen days were up, I took a cab to the nearest liquor store and, with a huge sigh, swallowed a pint of Johnnie Walker Red Label whisky. Not long after Harlem Hospital Center, I got connected to a Black woman and her husband in Brooklyn. We shot heroin together and participated in all kinds of depravity.

Endlessly looking for someone or something to satisfy my hollow soul, myself, I was wondering in darkness, unsure of what to do with my ruined life. In the midst of being numb most of the time, a splinter of hope still sprang to the surface of my mind and heart on occasion. With whatever was left, I took the splinter of hope and chose life.

Doctors, social services, and sparse numbers of people who were friendly toward me spoke strongly to me by their body language and facial expressions. The message said loudly and clearly:

"Don't trouble us anymore with your lies and actions; you have to figure this out by yourself. We are finished trying to help you."

The Power of Words and Labels

Labels are all around us. A label defines an individual or a group as a certain type of person or object. Labels are not neutral and can stick to us as though they were embedded in our DNA. Labels are a description of the contents of the person. Words mixed with beliefs become reality, whether we are told and believe we are smart, slow, angry, fun, caring, or distant. We conform to how others describe us, and that influences who we become and how we live. Words are another lie of the devil, who is defined as the author of lies.

Dad never controlled or filtered his speech, regularly spouting cruel, painful words to his family and everyone he judged. If a person was overweight, unattractive, or disagreed with his narcissistic perspective on life, he did not hesitate to verbalize his thoughts and feelings.

Words influence who we become. From birth to death, words form how we value ourselves and others. What comes out of our mouth brings death or life. The meaning of words shapes our attitudes, self-worth, and beliefs. Especially important are the words we speak to children. Communication involves the entire person and is a defining factor of humans. The meaning of words creates images in the mind and involves a shared interpretation and understanding. People can influence the destinies of their children by choosing the right words.

Words can determine whether a child is successful in life. Words meant to degrade or injure are like being stabbed with a sword that penetrates to the deepest parts. The wound slowly or never heals. Words spoken to us accumulate in our mind and soul like old newspapers or books that become cluttered and without order. Certain hormones are released, and stress is heightened when negative words are spoken. Using positive words promotes physical and emotional health and can bring hope and success. Words can cause suicide and wars and can be poison to the soul and mind. We have a need for words as much as we do for food and water. It does matter what others say because everyone desires to be known, heard, and understood. When you deceive someone, you present a false view of reality. Even those who believe they know the facts but have not verified them can influence another person's decisions. Opinions, attitudes, and beliefs are not always factual or accurate. It also states in Proverbs 15:1 (NIV) that "a gentle answer turns away wrath, but a harsh word stirs up anger." So when adults speak harshly to their children, it will result in anger that sometimes takes years to understand, as most children shove it deep into their soul. Do we deceive others with our speech by flattering them or name-calling that contributes to how they see the world, God, and self? Our words reveal what is in our heart.

The silent treatment and non-verbal communication is a passive-aggressive defense communication that can be more painful than words. Our body language, tone, and facial expressions can thunder loudly. Jesus is the alpha and omega, the total ultimate word, because He is the beginning and the end. On the cross Jesus received the ultimate silent treatment from God in our place. It may appear or feel like God is giving us the silent treatment when we suffer for a length of time or receive no answer to desperate prayers.

My fraternal grandmother had a look she gave you when she disapproved of what you said or of your behavior. There was no question about what she was saying, and attached to the distortion of her mouth was "and you better stop it now."

We are told in Genesis 1:1–3 that God spoke into existence the light, the waters, the sky, and all things that were part of creation. God spoke all things to life, including Adam and Eve. All relationships are formed by communication, which means to share or to make common. At the heart of all humanity is a system of meaning, what people believe and think.

> Each day we make many choices. We choose what we want to eat. We choose our friends. We choose our activities. We chose how we are going to behave. One of the big choices we make constantly is our choice of words. We choose what kind of words we are going to use.[vi]

The Lord gave Moses the words to speak to the people (Exodus 19:7). Psalm 12:6 (NIV) states, "And the words of the Lord are flawless, like silver purified in a crucible, like gold refined seven times." We are transformed and built up. The words of the Lord are always used for good to bring a person into fellowship and into His family. God always keeps His word, for Joshua 21:45 (NIV) says:

"Not one of all the LORD's good promises to Israel failed, everyone was fulfilled."

Jesus displayed His power by a blending of words and action. Jesus' identity as God qualified Him to use words in a powerful way. "Despite the power of Jesus' words over spirits, illness, and personified nature, Jesus embodies how this power is not meant for domination over people but rather to serve them."[vii] When the word of God comes into language, language itself is redeemed, and with it, man's relation to reality. Communication is irreversible, and it's indelible; a person can't erase what has been said. Communication involves the total personality—a person's communication cannot be separated from the person. It is a defining characteristic of a human being.

Jars are meant to be labeled, not people. Until a person accepts that he or she is believing and living out lies, a person becomes what he or she is labeled. Even attempts to build self-esteem in a person by telling him or her they can do anything and become anything he or she wants can be detrimental.

In our current culture, people are discredited and removed from social media for saying words deemed inappropriate. People making the judgment call on what words can and cannot be expressed are not objective; they have biases and agendas that influence who they allow to speak. We face a loss of freedom of speech as individuals, and corporations wield control of power on an impulse. Being intentional regarding communicating with friends and those we love is life-giving. Friends who have poured into our lives and saved us should be honored on a regular basis.

Time seemed to speed up, and by the time Meg and I connected again, we were both living in Southern California. I married Rick, a young man from college. I was able to work full time and earn two master's degrees. I graduated with a master's in religious education and, years later, a master's in marriage and family counseling. I was working as a hospice chaplain and in a substance abuse unit at a general hospital as a therapist and speaking at women's events.

"It's Meg," I hollered one day to my husband as I watched a TV commercial. There was Meg pouring milk into a bowl of multigrain cereal in a kitchen with a husband and children. A short time later, Meg was on a comedy series and played a woman involved with a dysfunctional family. Calling the actors guild that week, I talked to a man who said he'd pass my name onto Meg but understandably could not give me her contact information. Days later, I answered the phone.

"Barbara, it's Meg."

We talked for a couple of hours and discovered Meg was married with a young son and living in the San Fernando Valley. My husband, Rick, and I had a home in Orange County, about an hour from Meg. We reminisced, laughed, cried, and talked about our future.

"We're growing old together, Meg," I told her one day.

I believe Meg saved my life during times when I was oblivious to dangerous, life-threatening circumstances. One of the greatest moments Meg and I shared together was when she attended a party given for me when I graduated with my doctorate in ministry leadership. This was genuine friendship, and we continue to encourage and be present for one another. Graduating with a doctoral degree was miraculous. Early in my sobriety and Christian walk, some people believed I had brain damage and may not complete the one-year program. Graduating from Evangel University four years later, I was awarded the outstanding biblical student award and earned a grade point average of three point nine. My achievements educationally and in life reflect the healing power and love of God. My daily prayer is that God uses my story for His glory and to give hope and encouragement to others, no matter what labels and limits doctors and society place on them.

Jesus' power is exhibited in the Gospels in a blending of action and word. Jesus had authority over spirits, earthly elements, and healing and spoke into existence or being things that were not. He can raise the dead and cause a fig tree to die by His words. Just by the words or breath. Though Jesus' words have power over spirits, illness, and all creations, His power is not meant to dominate people but to serve them.

Genesis, the first book of the Bible, means "beginnings." God spoke creation into existence, including the human race. God never speaks in a demeaning manner to anyone. He is a God who builds up and speaks only the truth. Words have never meant more than they did in 2021. The overly sensitive culture was easily offended by speech and exclusive power given to certain words like "liberal" or "conservative" or "evangelical." What the words represent can elicit a multitude of eruptive or encouraging feelings and reactions. But who determines what words are "offensive"? It depends on your political and, many times, religious affiliation. People believe the lies spoken to them about God, society, and themselves. My father's words could be cruel, killing the inquisitiveness and motivation to set and achieve goals. Children's creativity and potential can be choked by parents, caretakers, teachers, or other influential adults who damage children by their speech. Dad made fun of my brother for pulling out his eyelashes as a young boy, calling him a freak and asking, "What is wrong with you?" The first step is people must understand they believe a lie when demeaning labels are used to describe them. People use words to control others and nations, and this happens in all aspects of life, causing physical or emotional and spiritual death. We have a need for words—like "food" or "water." We need to hear from others outside ourselves, whether negative or positive.

Proverbs 18:21 (NIV) says, "The tongue has the power of life and death, and those who love it will its fruit."

Both the Old and New Testaments in the Bible speak of the effect of words. Proverbs 12:18 says in The Message translation, "Rash language cuts and maims, but there is healing in the words of the wise." Proverbs 16:24 (MSG) says, "Gracious speech is like clover honey—good taste to the soul, quick energy for the body." In the New Testament, the book of John speaks of Jesus in the opening chapter. John is talking about Jesus and says, "The Word became flesh and made his dwelling among us. We have seen his glory, the glory of the one and only Son, who came from the Father, full of grace and truth" (John 1:14, NIV). Jesus is the word that came to earth to sacrifice His life for our sins. He took our punishment so we could be clean, free from the consequences of sin.

God is not limited by our past because our past does not define us. It is not an easy process, but we can recognize the people in our life who help us face our addiction and underlying issues as a gift. Facing the truth about me was tolerated only because I sensed His acceptance and forgiveness. Pain activated my impulse to run away, but I asked God to keep me as I daily surrendered to Him. As I marinated on God's words in the Bible, God became even more of a mystery to me. He was not a vindictive and punishing God, ready to catch my hand in the cookie jar. As I understood and looked to Jesus Christ, God's love became visible and exclusive in the cross. Guilty of my sins and deserving eternal death apart from a holy God, Jesus stepped in and took the bullet for me. It was the only means of connecting humans to God. He was the sinless lamb of God.

How could God forgive me when I could not forgive myself? It comes down to choosing to accept and personalize the sacrifice Jesus made for me and the world. That is the ultimate gift that gives us value. I have learned through the years that I am not what happened to me; I am so much more. God's love is based on our finding Him, but it is initiated by the Lord seeking us regardless of our status. The apostle Paul prays for us in Ephesians 3:14–19 (MSG):

> My response is to get down on my knees before the Father, this magnificent Father who parcels out all heaven and earth. I ask him to strengthen you by his Spirit—not a brute strength but a glorious inner strength—that Christ will live in you as you open the door and invite him in. And I ask him that with both feet planted firmly on love, you'll be able to take in with all followers of

Jesus the extravagant dimensions of Christ's love. Reach out and experience the breadth! Test its length! Plumb the depths! Rise to the heights! Live full lives, full in the fullness of God.

Brennan Manning says in his book *The Furious Longing of God*, "For His love is never, never, never based on our performance, never conditioned by our moods—of elation or depression. The furious love of God knows no shadow of alteration or change. It is reliable. And always tender."[viii]

On January 13, 1982, I watched as an Air Florida Boeing 737–222 plunged into the Potomac River in Washington, DC, killing seventy-eight people. Though the weather was bad, the plane took off after being deiced. With seventy-four passengers and five crew members, the plane took off after a forty-five-minute delay. Thirty seconds later, the plane crashed into the Fourteenth Street bridge over the Potomac River, less than a mile from the runway. Four motorists died driving over the bridge that was hit in by the plane. There were six survivors in the river, and two people emerged as heroes that day because they gave their life to rescue others and take them to safety. Williams survived the crash and passed lifelines on to others rather than take one for himself. He was the only passenger to die from drowning. The bridge was later renamed the Arland D. Williams Jr. Memorial Bridge. Jesus gave us a lifeline and took our place so we could live. The scene of Arland Williams and another man submerged underwater for the third and final time flashes through my mind on occasion. We fanaticize about how we hope we will react in a crisis where people's lives are at risk. I guess we never know for certain until an unwanted and unexpected emergency occurs. God knows what we face and is able to give us the grace to provide us the courage to glorify him.

The destiny of a terrible fate of judgment and hopelessness is replaced by a message of unconditional love and freedom.

"The drumbeats of doom in your head will be replaced by a song in your heart, which could lead to a twinkle in your eye. You will not be dependent on the company of others to ease your loneliness, for He is Emmanuel—God with us."[ix]

Insight: What have you used in your life to numb your pain? Relationships, chemicals, food, shopping, gambling or more?

Chapter 7:

Choose Life or Death

My first experience with death was attending my maternal grandfather's funeral at age four. I was curious about death and vaguely recall cautiously approaching Granddad's casket, gently reaching my hand out, and touching his face. After the funeral family and friends met for a buffet meal. I watched my grandmother reach for her handkerchief tucked in the pocket of her black chiffon dress each time someone came near her. The subdued and mournful environment confused me as circles of people laughed at Grandfather's sense of humor. Others were wiping tears away as they recounted his goodness. It was confusing to me, so I focused on the chocolate oatmeal cookies at the dessert table.

My fraternal grandfather died before I met him. Every other weekend our family visited the cemetery to place yellow daises on his grave. I didn't resist going because the cemetery was a great place to practice my cartwheels and play tag with my brother and cousin.

At age twelve my mom took my brother and me to the cemetery to teach us to drive using Dad's light green Cadillac. As long as we didn't run over the graves, Mom thought we were ready to drive, though we'd have to wait a few more years to make it legal.

Mom was a nurse on the pediatric unit at St. Luke's Hospital, and I would often ask her how many children died that week and how they died. I was inquisitive about God and death and what happened when a person died. Mom did the best she could to explain death and heaven and hell.

By age fifteen I was certain God wanted nothing to do with me. At the age of seventeen, I experienced regular panic attacks that produced a foreboding sense of death. "You're having panic attacks," a doctor informed me. "I'm going to give you some Valium, so when you feel an attack coming on, take one." I started using the pills daily along with alcohol, which was a dangerous combination and intensified alcoholic blackouts.

Feeling like age fifty at age twenty-two, I was living and working in New York City, where I managed a travel agency on Madison Avenue. As I opened the office door each morning, I feared that would be the day I lost my job because of frequent absenteeism and sloppy work ethic at times. One lonely Saturday afternoon, I called out to God, asking Him for help. Shame flooded my heart and mind, and nothing I did or put in my body took it away. I had a myriad of daily sins but hoped He might give me one more chance to pull my life together.

Possibly attending church regularly would please God, and perhaps I could learn how to live a purposeful, productive life. The next day I promised God and myself that I would get to a church service that day. While walking to get coffee, I strolled by a building with a sign that said "Chapel." As I neared the door, I could see people, so I walked in and went directly to the room with the stained glass windows and soft organ music playing. I sat there alone, believing I was early. A man walked in dressed in a black suit; he bent down and whispered in my ear, "What service are you here for?" I quickly responded, "Oh, I don't care, whatever one starts next." Waiting in silence, I prayed, "God, You probably want nothing to do with me, but I promise I will try and please You by changing my life. Please speak to me today, Lord, because I keep messing up."

Minutes later, two men pushed a silver casket with a large circle of white lilies, carnations, and hydrangeas flowing over the top at the front of the chapel. Shocked by the presence of the casket, I looked around and fled to the lobby and out the door. As I was opening the door, a man in a tan suit coat, navy trousers, and a blue striped tie gently put his hand on my shoulder and said, "Can I help you, ma'am? You look frightened, and you're shaking; come sit for a minute, and I'll get you some water." I sighed, sat in the chair, and realized I was in a mortuary chapel. Shaking my head from left to right, I said to myself, *Great, Barb, this is the message God has for you; it's over!* Smiling as he handed me a bottle of water with the funeral home name on the label, he asked:

"Did you just lose someone close to you?"

"No," I answered as I twisted off the cap and drank some water. "It's a huge mistake—that's all. I didn't know this was a funeral chapel. I was looking for a church to pray and hear from some kind of God out there." I stood up to leave and said, "Thanks for your help and the water."

"Wait...we're having a service Thursday evening for people who have lost a loved one at 7:00 p.m. I invite you to come."

"I haven't lost anyone." With arresting brown eyes and a calming smile, he said:

"Maybe you lost yourself."

Annoyed by his statement, I replied, "Well, if I lost myself, I sure wouldn't come to a mortuary to find me. I'm trying to live, not die!"

"Sometimes part of us needs to die to find life. God answers prayer in ways best for us," he said.

"I don't know what you mean, but thanks for inviting me."

That night I could not sleep thinking about this man; who was he, and what did he mean we have to die to live? The times I almost died flashed through my mind like a fast-forward movie. "How do I die to myself? I thought the caskets were telling me I was going die and take a forever trip to hell." How is a casket with a dead body in it a symbol of life?

Restlessness plagued me all day Thursday. I started to walk toward the funeral chapel around 7:00 p.m. that night. Slowly pulling the heavy glass door open, I peeked in the lobby. No one was there, so I tiptoed into the chapel and sat in the last row. There was a panel in the front of the chapel of two women and a man who were answering questions from the twenty-five or so people about grief, loss, and death. The majority were women who held packets of Kleenex as they listened. One woman asked, "My twenty-year-old son just died of alcoholism and drug addiction a month ago. His father and I tried to get him help several times, but he always went back to that life; he was never able to get free from the dope or the drink. My heart is broken, and I don't know if I'll ever survive. I can't believe such a smart and happy child is dead and that death could have been avoided. It's such a waste of life. What do you recommend for my family? How do we get through this?" The panel gave resources and pamphlets on working through the death of a child who died due to drugs or alcohol.

I didn't hear all the answers to her questions because I couldn't take my eyes off this mother. All I could hear were the words, "It was a wasted life." The man who'd invited me leaned over and whispered, "It's good to see you; would you like to talk after the event?" I nodded yes.

The man met me in the lobby and directed me to an office behind the small flower shop. He pulled out a chair for me and sat a few feet away in a large office chair.

"Who are you? What's your name, and why are you taking an interest in me?"

Smiling, he answered, "My name is Virgil Gabriel, and I work for the mortuary as a grief counselor and community resource person. I do other jobs, but those are my two main positions here. I saw pain in your face, Barbara, when you mistakenly came to our chapel looking for a church service. God has strange ways of answering prayer and sends people to us we may not ordinarily seek out ourselves. I believe He knows what we need."

"I don't believe in God," I answered. "He's never been there when I needed Him, and I don't think He wants anything to do with me because of all the horrible sins I've committed. People have disappointed me much of my life, but I've also manipulated and used others for my own selfish needs."

"But you prayed, right, Barbara? So you must believe in some kind of God?"

"I'm desperate," I answered. "I'll be lying upfront here in one of those caskets with my hands folded over the satin trim of my pink death dress. I want a different life; I just can't do it!"

"Maybe that's the problem; you've been trying to change by grit and self-will. We all need other people, and I believe the love and power of a higher power I call God can and will help you. I can see the pain in your eyes, Barbara. It tells me you are disillusioned and hardened from betrayals and your own choices. I challenge you to take a risk and trust someone again, someone who can help you discover freedom. Remember when I told you sometimes we have to die to live? I meant that you have to die to fear and your own need for control, which is just an illusion anyway. I'm talking about a surrender of self to God and others who will walk by you in your process of transformation. It's possible, Barbara, but it requires courage and determination."

"I don't know; where do I start? It seems too overwhelming, and I always fail."

He smiled and handed me a card with a woman's name who he believed would help me.

"But I don't have the money for a therapist," I said as I offered back his card.

"Don't worry; she will not charge you. She is a counselor and mentor who volunteers her time with women who need help."

I looked more closely at the card and saw the name Angela Mary Davidson.

"Okay, I'll call her and see. Thanks, Mr. Gabriel. I'll let you know how things turn out."

"I'd like that," he said, walking me to the door. The next morning, I called the number.

"Hello, Mrs. Davidson. I was referred to you by Virgil Gabriel from Community Funeral Chapel. He said you might be open to talking to me. I've talked with some counselors over the years, but I wasn't ready to hear what they said and not ready to start the process of changing my life. It was as though I sabotaged the smallest of successes, not feeling that I deserved to get sober or to be happy. I believed it was impossible for me to change. Counseling and twelve-step groups work for others, but I just couldn't stick with them. I felt more and more hopeless."

"Barbara, do you want to live or die? If you want to live, I can help you not just survive but really live a meaningful life."

"I guess I want to live, Mrs. Davidson, or I wouldn't be calling you. I don't know who I am or how to change, and I'm so terrified of dying. When I ended up in the mortuary chapel, believing it to be a church chapel, I realized God was speaking to me about choosing life or death while I was still able. I think I believe in heaven and hell. I want to live, but I've disappointed God, my family, and myself beyond forgiveness.

"Barbara, I'm going to send you to a colleague of mine for evaluation. He won't charge you, but I'd like his opinion." As she handed me his card, she said, "He's a psychiatrist, and his name is Dr. Quinten Hyder."

"See another psychiatrist? I don't think that will help."

"Wait a minute. You committed to taking my direction, correct?"

"Okay, I'll go." That week I had an appointment with the doctor.

With his hands folded on his desk and in a somber voice, Dr. Hyder said:

"You won't live to see your next birthday if you don't get help."

I knew he was correct, and I'd die if I continued making such destructive decisions. I felt like a wild animal ambushed and caged, unable to get away. But where would I go, and what was I running from? Just myself, and it was time to stop. "If you are interested, here is the name and number of a program for women outside of New York City." He handed me the number on the back of his card.

"I have no insurance or money left for treatment," I replied quickly, dismissing the possibility.

"It doesn't require insurance or money, just a willingness to change." I'd never heard of such a thing...how and why would people help an alcoholic/addict without money?

Weeks later, I woke up in a psychiatric unit in queens. I wasn't sure how I got there but suspected I had had another alcoholic blackout. I understood I was facing impending death if something didn't change. Sitting in a small room where we were allowed to smoke, a woman across from me was vigorously snuffing out her cigarette and said to herself while shaking her head:

"I should have stayed at that home."

Touching the sleeve of her hospital gown, I asked:

"What home are you talking about?" "Oh, it's a Christian program for women addicts and alcoholics outside the city in Garrison.

"It's called The Walter Hoving Home."

The following day the doctor released me with a prescription for more tranquilizers. I was renting a room in a house in Queens and glad to be back in my tiny room. The older couple who owned the home wondered where I'd been the past few days. Of course, I made up a crazy story and did not ask further questions. I knew they were suspicious and beginning to speculate what was wrong. It was only a matter of time before I was kicked out. As I lay on the bed, I played the video in my head of the past two years. Something or someone was keeping me alive because, on several occasions, I should have died. Maybe Mom's prayers reached God. As I pulled out the papers from the hospital, I saw Dr. Hyder's card on the floor. On the back I read the name of the facility he suggested for a one-year program. It was the same name the woman I smoked with in the hospital said she wished she'd stayed, The Walter Hoving Home. I ran to the phone and called, and a pleasant-sounding woman answered, "Hello, this is Shirley with The Walter Hoving Home. How can I help you?"

After a short assessment, she said, "Barbara, we'd love to have you in our program. You can come tomorrow; will you do that?"

"Oh yes, I'll be there."

That night after drinking, I went to the emergency room and lied about a diagnosis so I could have a shot of the painkiller Demerol. As I continued to procrastinate daily, Shirley finally said:

"Come today, Barb, or don't come."

The next twenty-four hours were foggy, but somehow I packed what little I had and called Arthur.

"Hi, Arthur. Can you please drive me to Garrison this morning? If I don't go into this program, I will die."

Arthur was a young man I'd worked with and who loved me deeply. I used and manipulated him because he was convenient and was easily persuaded.

"I'll pick you up after I take the truck back around eleven."

That day I entered The Walter Hoving Home (The New York Girls Teen Challenge) and spent the next four days detoxing from lethal levels of various drugs and alcohol. Shortly after arriving, I was told I became unconscious and drifted in and out of a comatose state. The director's son carried me upstairs to a room during the day, and I slept downstairs on the couch in the large living room at night with staff and girls in the program praying for me during the night. I've been told I was close to death. On the fifth day, I woke in a cold sweat, and someone handed me a can of Sprite, which I drank without stopping. I was extremely dehydrated physically, emotionally, and spiritually. I was advised to drink as much water as possible. A woman with a broad smile stood over me.

"Do you feel well enough to get up, Barbara?"

Adjusting my vision, I said, "Yes, I think so."

She helped me up and introduced me to a short, thin lady named Angie. Angie would be my "big sister" and help me get adjusted. Angie was an Italian from Brooklyn who had been there for four months. It sounded like she said, "Hey Bob" (that's Barb in Brooklynite). The following days I was assigned to a room with Angie and began to eat and took a much-needed bath. It was December, and the snow was knee-deep. A beautifully decorated Christmas tree stood in the corner of the living room next to a large glass window and door to a patio. Why was everyone so nice to me? They were people I didn't know, and if they knew me, they wouldn't be so welcoming. A sense of peace and happiness seemed to seep through the walls of this home. Later I would come to understand that it was the love and power of Jesus that dwelt in that place.

There is a saying that states, "There are no atheists in fox holes," because when you are in the middle of a war in which you may die, life becomes a gift you don't want to let go of or lose. The God who has been denied suddenly becomes the source of your hope and focus of prayer. God has ways to get our attention so that we might know the God who created us and also gave us our identity. Believing I needed to be more presentable in order to come to God, I promised I'd clean up my life. (God knew I hadn't kept a promise in years.)

God's heart tenderly responded with, "You can't clean up your life, but if you let Me be part of your life, I'll clean it up." Could the voice of the Lord be speaking to me? Would God actually communicate in a personal way with me?

After a couple of months at the Home, I was filled with astonishment to learn about living water that would transform my life. Jesus declared in John 7:37–38 (NIV), "On the last and greatest day of the festival, Jesus stood and said in a loud voice, 'Let anyone who is thirsty come to me and drink. Whoever believes in me, as Scripture has said, rivers of living water will flow from within them.'" And a promise in Revelation 7:17 (NIV) provides a snapshot glimpse of eternity. It states, "For the Lamb at the center of the throne will be their shepherd; 'he will lead them to springs of.' 'And God will wipe away every tear from their eyes.'"

Before I could begin to comprehend God's truth and apply it to my life, I went through a time of adjusting to the rigorous daily schedule and requirements. Living in a Christian environment with every hour filled with classes, prayer time, work time, or personal devotions was precisely what I needed. After a few weeks, I was able to settle in and adapt.

It was a Monday night prayer meeting, and I could hear the director's wife playing the piano and people singing. As I entered the small chapel, I froze momentarily as I heard and watched people raise their arms and worship God. Some spoke in a language I'd never heard before. Fear swept over me, and with the hair lifting on my arms and the nape of my neck, I ran out of the room. In the living room was a phone booth encased in mahogany wood that matched the interior of the house. I closed the door and called a friend collect.

"You got to get me out of here." I was barely able to speak; I was in such a panic.

"I think these people are in a trance, and they are going to offer me up as a sacrifice or something! No wonder they don't want money."

My friend was able to calm me down and encouraged me to return to the service and talk to someone. Though I wanted to trust God and the people, anxious doubts climbed barriers and slithered into my mind and soul and rested there.

With that advice I spoke to Shirley, the counselor who approved my entrance into the program. From that night on, it was a process of learning about worshipping God and giving thanks in song and speaking the Word of God.

Weeks later, I knelt at the cross at an evening prayer meeting and prayed. Unable to fully describe it, I stood up feeling as though spiritual bleach had just cleansed my soul. No therapist or drug or relationship or amount of money could cause me to feel like I did when I got off my knees. An electrified sense of hope and pureness permeated my entire being and the room. In the next weeks, I began to make sense of why the blood of Jesus was necessary in order for me to be forgiven of sins. People have commented that Christianity is a bloody religion and should be for peace—there is enough war and brutality in the world. But they do not understand the means to legitimate, lasting peace comes at a price because of the gravity of sin. It is established on the word "covenant." People are clueless about the word and its significance; it is a recurring pattern throughout the Bible. Animals were sacrificed in the Old Testament covenants for the forgiveness of the sins of the people. Leviticus 17:11 (NIV) in the Old Testament states that "For the life of a creature is in the blood and I have given it to you to make atonement for yourselves on the altar; it is the bold that makes atonement for one's life." Sin is so serious to God, who will not change, and blood must pay the price. God is merciful but holy and just. God's holiness does not allow Him to look at sin. Hebrews 9:22 (NIV) says:

"In fact, the law requires that nearly everything be cleansed with blood, and without the shedding of blood there is no forgiveness." Jesus, who was fully God and fully man, was the only one who could permanently bridge the gap between man and God forever. Animal sacrifices are no longer required because Jesus entered the throne room of God and took our punishment on Himself so we can be forgiven once for evermore. He took our sin and gave us His righteousness. Immediately before He died, Jesus said, "It is finished." The blood of bulls and goats is no longer required to cleanse people from sin, but only by coming to God through Jesus' shed blood on the cross can we stand before God. By accepting Jesus' substitutionary death and the spilling of His own blood, we stand before God, covered with the righteousness of Christ.

Believing and stating that I felt forgiven by Jesus' sacrifice and blood seemed absurd in a logical and finite world, but inside it was as though a door in my heart and soul that had been bolted shut for years had been unlocked and opened. Convinced the room was full of darkness, poisonous snakes, and oversized rats, I feared opening it. The repulsive smell of the accumulation of my life's mistakes and sin would be too suffocating and overpowering. But Jesus asked me if He could unlock the door, and I agreed. He stood in front of me as an act of protection and love. As Jesus unbolted the locked door, He opened it slightly to ease my fear. He entered the room and asked me to follow. Brushing away the cobwebs, He removed a shield on the window. Light started to enter the cluttered room, and He opened the tightly locked window. Fresh air replaced the stale dirty smell, and Jesus said, "Barbara, this room is usable; all that has frightened you and was hidden is cleared away. Let's decorate it and spend time together. You see, 'I stand at the door and knock, and if you hear my voice and open the door, I will come in and we will share a meal together as friends'" (Revelation 3:20, NLT). Though self-awareness and healing occurred that day, God would continue spiritual and emotional surgery in the future. There was an abundance of work to do in the rooms of my heart and soul, but this was a beginning I had never conceived possible. It is counterintuitive to be gifted with acceptance, forgiveness, and unconditional love from a holy God without retribution and punishment. Too inconceivable for our finite minds. We can marvel and be humbled that Jesus Christ took our punishment so we can be free.

Developing the discipline of prayer and Bible reading was the foundation of building a new life. I memorized a passage of scripture per week, and the Holy Spirit stirred within me, personalizing God's truth. I learned the Holy Spirit is not a force or ghost but the third person of the Trinity. There was no question the Bible was alive and able to penetrate the hardest heart. Learning basic life skills such as responding appropriately to anger and disappointment, being responsible as an adult to pay bills on time, and resolving conflict were incorporated in the program. Not knowing my personal preferences, such as my favorite color, food, music, or leisure activity, contributed to the fact that I knew little about myself.

About the second month there, I was called into the director's office during a class. I opened the door and saw two men dressed in suits sitting across the desk from the director. Shirley invited me to sit down and began to tell me the two men were from the Secret Service and they were there to see me. Both handsome young men introduced themselves and began to tell me I was in trouble. In my insanity, I plotted to start a revolution and threatened to kill the president of the United States. Taking a deep breath, I swallowed and sat there motionless. Unable to clarify or provide details as to why I did such a foolish act, I admitted to the charges and completed the paperwork they requested. "We'll be talking with the attorney general, but if you stay in this program, you may not have to face charges and go to jail." Though they made no promises or guarantees, Shirley prayed with me after the men left, and the sobering reality of the consequences of my choices and behaviors haunted me for weeks. I plotted ways I could escape the country and avoid going to jail. My grandiose thinking and planning soon collapsed as I faced the reality of no money or place to go. God saved my life, and I needed to do the right thing and face the repercussions. Learning to surrender outcomes to the Lord was the only solution. I was not in control and never was because being in control is only an illusion.

Toward the beginning of my fourth month at the Home, I began to feel extremely tired and sick. My skin and eyes started to have a yellow tint, so I was taken to a clinic. I was told I had contracted hepatitis B from a dirty needle while shooting heroin. Scenes flashed in my mind as I shuttered at the memories and the penalties to my health. A drug and alcohol program is an inconvenient place to be physically sick. I shared a large room with three other girls who were assigned to bring me meals and schoolwork; otherwise, I was confined to bed. Two staff members suggested I go home to Florida because Mom was a nurse, and I could return when I was better. "Please let me stay," I pleaded. "I know I'll never get back here, and I will die." They agreed to allow me to stay, and I consciously stayed out of the way, making no extra requests or work for the girls.

During my restricted time in bed, I observed many sounds and sights and new loves. Across the Hudson River was West Point Military Academy, where we could hear taps playing. West Point educated the country's finest men and women, and on the other side was the Lord's academy, preparing women to return to their families and fight the good fight of faith in a troubled world.

A small grayish-black miniature poodle named Mitsy lived down the road from the Home but seldom stayed home. Daily Mitsy skipped through the woods from her home and spent her days and sometimes nights with the women at the Home. Mitsy believed she was a guard dog and didn't back down from dogs much larger. She believed in herself and felt one of her purposes was to protect the home and help the groundskeeper with daily tasks of the upkeep of the property. Mitsy encouraged and amused me with her antics of bringing me gifts of small tree branches. I taught her a couple of typical dog commands; she would sit, put out her paw when I said shake, and bark when I asked her to speak. I'd like to believe Mitsy knew I needed her because she faithfully came to my room daily at about the same time.

I fell in love with this small, scraggly canine who had the biggest brown eyes. This began my love affair with dogs.

The home was located on a hill with twenty-seven acres of beautiful woods and creeks and surrounded by a stone wall in Garrison, New York, about two hours from Manhattan. It had a long winding gravel road that led to the main house and a number of other buildings. The facility was a former home for retired railroad engineers in the middle of lush trees, creeks, and foliage. The picturesque estate was quiet and the perfect place for reflection, prayer, exercise, and conversational walks. Walter Hoving, who at the time was the chairman of Tiffany's in New York City, referred the director to a foundation that paid the mortgage annually until it was paid in full. The foundation wanted the home named after Mr. Hoving and understood it would be a Christian program for women with drug and alcohol abuse issues. It was established in 1967 and was part of the New York Girl's Teen Challenge Center. Teen Challenge was a program for gang members started by Pastor David Wilkerson and affiliated with the Assemblies of God denomination. The Walter Hoving Home was established around 1967 as a one-year residential program. An Assemblies of God–ordained minister, Reverend John Benton, and his wife, Elsie, were the first directors and remained president and CEO for fifty years. Bear Mountain near Garrison was a popular tourist location with gorgeous views and impressive ski resorts.

In 2017 I attended the fifty-year anniversary of the Walter Hoving Home in New York, along with a group of alumni I graduated with from the Home. Present at the gala event was Walter Hoving's grandson. He spoke, and I was profoundly affected by his testimony. He had become an alcoholic and spent years struggling with his alcoholism. He got sober over ten years ago and is now a practicing psychologist in New York City, working primarily with people battling addictions. Walter Hoving planted seeds into a substance abuse program to help women with alcohol and drug dependency over forty years earlier. Mr. Hoving was unaware that his own grandson would require treatment for an addiction years later. I believe when we plant seeds to help others, especially in Christ's name, we reap blessings.

Proverbs 11:25 (NIV) says, "A generous person will prosper; whoever refreshes others will be refreshed."

The amazing principle of the gospel is we get to continue to pass the good news forward as we share our story of Jesus' redeeming act at the cross and His resurrection from the dead.

The central message in the gospel is to love others and give sacrificially. As we serve others, we serve the Lord and honor Him. Even Jesus said, "I have come to serve, not to be served" (Matthew 20:28). It is difficult to grasp that God Himself comes as a servant and becomes our role model.

A sign of Christian growth is when a person focuses on helping others rather than being self-absorbed. I recognized God was actively working in my life because I began to receive an abundance of joy in giving to others rather than focusing on my own needs and desires. Looking upward to the Lord and outward to others produces riches far greater than tangible wealth.

Soon it was my turn to sit up and pray for ladies who were detoxing from alcohol and drugs. Without much recognition I observed I was starting to be responsible. The staff could trust me to drive ladies to appointments and to complete tasks assigned to me. Soon I found myself in greater positions of leadership, assisting in training the ladies to be big sisters to new women in their first thirty days. Gratification as a result of caring for others and sacrificing in order to give permeated my heart and soul. Loving God and others is genuine lasting gratification and immeasurably more satisfying.

The daily schedule included morning devotions, classes on learning the Bible, topics like forgiveness, coping with fear and conflict, and the importance of modesty. The afternoon consisted of assigned work crews, dinner, and then class in the evening or group prayer. Hard work and daily structure were important in forming new habits, and most of the women were ready to sleep when lights went out at 9:30 p.m.

I developed close friendships at The Walter Hoving Home and continue to remain connected to those friends and staff members. As an ordained minister with the Assemblies of God and a seminary graduate, I have had the privilege in the years following my time to water baptize women from The Walter Hoving Home in Pasadena, California. Another meaningful event I shall cherish forever was being asked to officiate the funerals of two former staff members who had an enormous influence in my life from the day I entered the Home.

In the first year or two after graduating from the Home, I was rigid about keeping "the rules" and would confess if I accidentally broke a rule. Being so out of control all those years, I found safety and security in being relatively legalistic. The pendulum had to swing in the opposite direction, but eventually I found the balance between the law and grace. The realization that Jesus died in my place was the difference, and the fact that I was given His grace was revolutionary. The apostle Paul writes to the church at Rome that we are justified by faith alone.

The life-altering experiences that produced positive transformation were remarkable. I recall when I first started to have a sense of self-awareness. I felt like I was "born-again" in every aspect of my life—as though I was growing up all over again but in God's fast track. It has been stated in research that when a person begins to use substances on a regular basis, he or she ceases to develop and mature emotionally. I did not know what my favorite color was or if I had a favorite color. God has built into us patterns of emotional development, stages that we go through in developing as healthy, mature people. Hurts and emotional pain interrupt this process and cause us to remain stifled in development. God's grace and forgiveness build a base upon which a solid foundation allows for healthy development and realization. Though growth is a long-term process that takes a lifetime, God can accelerate the process in a person who has been discounted and their voice silenced for most of his or her life. Willpower and trying to be a better person do not work. What empowers us to change is God's unconditional love. The Bible states in 1 John 4:17–18 in The Message translation:

> God is love. When we take up permanent residence in a life of love, we live in God and God lives in us. This way, love has the run of the house, becomes at home and mature in us, so that we're free of worry on Judgment Day—our standing in the world is identical with Christ's. There

is no room in love for fear. Well-formed love banishes
fear. Since fear is crippling, a fearful life—fear of death,
fear of judgment—is one not yet fully formed in love.

Detoxing the body from harmful chemicals and removing
addictive behaviors are only the beginning of life in recovery. Alcohol,
drugs, and addictive behaviors are the symptoms of brokenness,
loneliness, and shame. It is the mechanism a person chooses to numb
and cope with pain. As God unfolds a person's past before him or her
in order to heal the fragmented pieces of a person's life, regret, shame,
and unworthiness work to steal hope. This is a common technique
the devil uses to try one more time to destroy the person. Accepting
God's forgiveness and forgiving self can be a distressing and agonizing
experience. From childhood a person is endowed with the awareness
that to be a good person one needs to work hard and not do harm to
others.

Earning love and approval seems to be embedded in a person's
DNA, and people believe there are little sins and big sins. But to God
every sin is the same, and if criminal, there is a price to pay. Nothing
in a person can secure a place at the pearly gates of heaven. No one can
do enough good deeds to earn salvation. Every human being wears a
robe of filthy sin until Jesus exchanges robes and gives us His robe
of righteousness and puts on our robe of sin. It's not about joining a
church or religion; it's about a reconciled relationship through Jesus
to God our Father.

Before He died on the cross, Jesus said, "It is finished." Once and
for all, sin had been atoned for through His death and resurrection.

Second Corinthians 5:21 (NIV) says, "God made him [Jesus] who had no sin to be sin for us, so that in him we might become the righteousness of God." That is how you get to heaven.

The apostle Paul reminded the Galatian church in the book of Galatians that man is justified by faith in Jesus Christ—nothing less and nothing more. "I do not set aside the grace of God, for if righteousness could be gained through the law, Christ died for nothing!" (Galatians 2:21, NIV).

Forgiving self is a painful and challenging process. Christ's work on the cross is counterintuitive in a culture that is based on obtaining a reward based on what a person produces. The need to earn love and acceptance seems to be embedded in a person's DNA. But the more I meditated and memorized Scripture, the more a deeper sense of freedom and faith settled in my soul. As I grew spiritually and emotionally, my focus turned outward toward the well-being and needs of others and away from myself. It's a biblical principle that when we give to others, we are satisfied. One of the Old Testament proverbs says, "A generous person will prosper; whoever refreshes others will be refreshed" (Proverbs 11:25, NIV). Marinating on the Bible produces healthy spiritual food that builds faith and increases intimacy with God. The powerful delicacies of the Word are to be shared with the world as we invite people to the table. Psalm 34:8 (NIV) says, "Taste and see that the Lord is good, blessed is the one who takes refuge in him."

The daily routine at the Home required hard work and a desire for a changed life. The staff lived on the grounds, and they were dedicated to the many women who came through the welcoming doors of the home. Not always understanding staff decisions that affected the ladies at the Home required willingness to yield my own will and logic. Late one night, while I had finally gotten into my REM sleep, I felt someone tap me on the shoulder and ask, "Barb, you were in the kitchen this afternoon, correct?" "Yes, I was." "Well, you didn't take the trash out, so please get up and do that." I glanced at the hall clock on my way to the kitchen; it was 10:30 p.m. As I tied up the large bag of trash and took it to the bin, I wondered why Frances had to wake me to do this; I'm sure she knew the demands of our day with little free time.

A short time later, I understood the significance of Frances waking me to complete the task I missed. A resolve to complete responsibilities was a character trait The Walter Hoving Home made a priority for the ladies.

Alcoholics and drug addicts have a propensity to live in extremes and to occupy a place where chaos is alive and active or isolate from everyone. We are either very good or very bad and seldom content in the middle. But in time routine and the simplicity of a disciplined life produce security and peace.

Years later, I worked with a young man who was a daily drinker and marijuana user. He ate sugar, rarely exercised, and smoked over a pack of cigarettes a day. The day he transferred from detox to the thirty-day program, he began a regiment of dramatically tearing up his cigarettes and tossing them, exercising, and eating only vegetables. I counseled him to the dangers of giving up everything at one time.

Unfortunately, he was not willing to take direction and started drinking and smoking weed and taking pills a week after he was discharged. It is crucial to take direction from others no matter how old we are chronologically, especially those who go before us and are living in recovery and practicing managing a daily healthy lifestyle.

Early in my faith at The Walter Hoving Home, I was of the opinion that Christians were dull, boring, and definitely lacked a sense of humor. The lens of my perception changed as I lived with and interacted with Christians. The program at the Home was intense, and we were challenged to recognize and face the truth of our past and the consequences of our choices. Some ladies who continually broke the rules were asked to leave. There were weeks I cried daily, feeling shame, regret, and worthlessness. But the good days increased with time, and personalizing the curriculum assigned to us in classes was monumental. The identification I felt with certain women of the Bible heightened my hunger to know more. Jesus engaged the Samaritan woman at the well who was living with a man, not her husband, which was culturally unorthodox. He saw her potential, and she became the first Samaritan evangelist, and her encounter with Him transformed her life for eternity. Jesus' attention to the woman with the flow of blood for twelve years left her segregated and quarantined. Jesus, a rabbi, allowed this unclean woman to touch Him without fear or apprehension of becoming unclean Himself. Instead Jesus healed her physically, emotionally, and spiritually. The twelve seemingly endless years with little hope of getting well disappeared in a moment with a touch for the healer.

Tears were healing, but so was laughter. I discovered that God had a remarkable sense of humor (just look at some of your family members, friends, and animals...and in the mirror). I mean, what was God thinking when He created a platypus? Psalm 126:2 (NIV) says, "Our mouths were filled with laughter, our tongues with songs of joy. Then it was said among the nations, 'The Lord has done great things for them.'"

Not living with Christians before, I carefully observed everything the leadership said and did.

Do they really live out what they say they believe? I asked myself. John Benton, the director of the program, was a generous man and, on occasion, took the entire staff to dinner at an elaborate restaurant. One evening, as dressed in, they all went out, and I decided I would monitor their actions when they returned. I did not believe people could go to dinner and not drink alcohol, whether wine or hard liquor. Because I was asked to monitor one of the residences, I approached two staff members as they arrived home with questions about a girl. The director, Shirley, had multiple sclerosis and parked near the main building. My plan was to get close enough and smell the person's breath to see if they had drunk alcohol. As I spoke I got close to Shirley, who was a former alcoholic in the New York bowery years before. No scent of alcohol, and I was relieved. I wanted to believe these people were sincere and lived what they professed. The Bible does not say not to drink alcohol, but it does warn us not to be drunk with wine (Ephesians 5:17).

On another occasion I was in the car with Elsie and John Benton driving back to the Home from visiting a church and sharing my testimony. We were in the midst of a February blizzard, and the glimmering, fast-falling snow made it difficult to see. The Home is in a more rural area with winding two-lane highways. The car heater was on high, and thinking about the warm bed waiting for me caused me to pray to myself, *Lord, get us back to the Home soon. I'm freezing.* As the car turned one of the final curves before reaching the Home, there was a small station wagon parked on our side of the road in an old gas station that was closed. Though there was little lighting, I could see a man and a woman in the front seat. I felt the car slow down and thought, *Certainly he's not going to pull over to help these people in this blast of ice and snow.* The car turned and stopped beside the other car. I watched Rev. Benton button the top button of his heavy coat and go to the driver's side of the car. It took about twenty-five minutes to change the tire as both men worked together. He brushed off his coat and stomped his feet to minimize the snow he'd bring inside the car. As I was pulling up the covers that night and moving my toes in the warm bed, laying my head down, I asked myself, *Why would someone stop and help a stranger in a blizzard like that?* As I grew in my faith and relationship with Christ, I knew the answer. When a person declares he or she is a follower of Jesus, others watch what you say and do, even the simplest reactions. The Bentons lived in a simple house on the property with their three children. The two girls, Marji and Connie, and the boy, Jim Benton, participated in most of the activities at the Home. They attended the prayer meetings and contributed to the family atmosphere. As adults, the Benton children became leaders in the church and in their families. Living in proximity to the women in the program provided a reality that gave each of the children a sensitivity and education about the human condition and alcohol and drug addiction. They also participated in witnessing the transformation of these otherwise discarded women. Compassion-filled with hope, each Benton adult has occupied a leadership position in a variety of ministries.

The director's wife, Elsie Benton, better known as Mom B, was a critical and necessary ingredient in creating a home-style environment for the women. When she walked into a room, an invigorating breath of fresh air followed. "Hi, Barb. How are you today?" she asked as her arms pulled me close for a big hug. This was not a sterile program like many of the programs the women had known. Mom B's cheerful and warm-hearted spirit put a smile on my face on days I felt lonely or apprehensive about my future. She was serious about the Word of God and her faith. She had wisdom and wasn't shy about confronting the women when necessary. Through the years Elsie Benton and I visited my hometown in Cedar Rapids, Iowa, where we spoke at a church and stayed for two days. It was the home where I was conceived and where my father now lived. Elsie was gracious and kind toward my dad, whose alcoholism had caused him to be irrational at times. I was embarrassed that the house had not been maintained or cleaned properly. Her humility and gratefulness made it easier to show her the small bed she would sleep in during our time there. It was my grandmother's bed that had been in the same spot for, no doubt, a hundred years. "Barb, don't apologize for giving me your grandmother's bed; we were missionaries in Japan and spent a multitude of nights sleeping on the floor." Smiling wide, Elise said, "Now, we are missionaries here in Cedar Rapids, Iowa. Just thank the Lord we can serve your dad and be examples of God's character to him and others."

I slept in a hideaway bed I used as a toddler, and the mattress springs poked me from my neck to my feet. I did not want to contemplate how many generations of dust mites called those mattresses home.

As the time for me to complete the one-year program approached, I experienced anxiety, not knowing what I was to do or where I should go. A couple of graduates from the Home were attending an Assemblies of God liberal arts university in Springfield, Missouri, and I was encouraged to investigate attending the same school.

I chuckled and thought, *I didn't even graduate reform school.* Though I had my GED, I had not done well in school and believed I was not competent to attend college. But God began to challenge me in a gentle but strong manner about trusting Him.

It was decided I would go directly to my mother and stepfather's home in Florida. They both loved the Lord and were rooted and grounded in the Bible and in a great church.

With a dry mouth and a stomach full of butterflies, I watched as the director announced the names of the graduates. I was amazed that I was alive and didn't die, and it was even more miraculous that I completed the one-year program. I had not finished much in my life except a bottle of vodka or a bag of drugs. It was my turn to speak and receive my certification of completion. My knees were shaking as I walked to the podium in the chapel. Biting my lip, I spoke openly and gratefully of how Christ changed my life. He gave me new desires and a peace of mind I had never experienced. I knew this was just the beginning of walking down a new road, and I feared I might fail God and others. But the Holy Spirit assured me of His presence, and as it states in the final verse of Psalm 23, verse 6 (NIV), "Surely your goodness and love will follow me all the days of my life and I will dwell in the house of the Lord forever."

After the graduation service, a meal was served, and I shared sad and happy memories with the women who had recently arrived and those who had become my friends.

After finishing the last bite of the scrumptious lemon-filled graduation cake, I walked down the hill with Frances, one of the counselors. I was uncertain about what I was going to do after I arrived at home. My immediate plan was to stay with my mom and stepdad, Dale, and find a job. They were delighted to have me come, and I could attend Bible study with them as well as stay as long as I wanted. Kicking a rock down the gravel driveway, I said, "Frances, I never even graduated reform school; how can I go to college?" "God can and will make a way, Barb. Put things out there and see what door the Lord opens."

Two days later, one of the ladies drove me to LaGuardia Airport bound for Fort Lauderdale, Florida. Smiling as she dropped me off, she said, "Stay in touch, Barb." "Oh, I will." I really wanted to say, "Don't leave me here." Looking around at all the people, I wanted to flee, but instead, I went to the bathroom. Juggling my luggage out of the small bathroom door contributed to my anxiety.

I stopped in my tracks; my brain felt paralyzed as I remembered that I hated to fly. I hadn't been in a plane for a couple of years and always had a marguerite or two before takeoff.

I stopped to lean against the wall at Anthony's Pizza. "God, since I'm not going to drink, You'll have to soothe my fear. Put someone next to me I can talk with because I'm going to trust You with my life and the life of everyone on board." Forgetting how noisy airports were, the chatter of people scrambling to get to their gates caused me to feel overwhelmed, so I hurried to the gate.

I got an aisle seat, and before getting comfortable, a woman with black hair and nicely dressed smiled and said, "Excuse me." I got up, and she sat next to me. After putting her bag under the seat in front of her, she said, "I really don't like to fly," as she fastened her seatbelt. I smiled. "I don't either." While the plane was gaining speed down the runway, she grabbed my hand. "Do you mind?" I squeezed her hand and said, "Not at all."

After reaching thirty-two thousand feet, she released my hand. "I'm Lorraine, Lorraine Schwartz. I'm on my way to Miami to open an office for my husband, who is a podiatrist on Park Avenue." I introduced myself and began to tell her about the last year at The Walter Hoving Home and how Jesus Christ saved me from death. Lorraine asked what my plans were now that I had completed the program. Sheepishly I told her I was thinking about a college in Missouri, though I stated I did not think I was college material. Our conversation continued, and soon we heard, "We are starting our approach to Fort Lauderdale airport, so please fasten your seatbelts." Sandwiched between passengers, we found our way into the airport. Lorraine went in the opposite direction to catch her ride to Miami.

Mom, my stepfather, Dale, and my brother, Greg, met me with hugs and smiles. I crawled in the back of the Pontiac LeMans and sat close to Greg. I talked about graduation, meeting Lorraine, and my prayers about college. "I don't think I'd make it in college. I never liked school and didn't do well." "Well, honey," Mom responded, "let's see what God has planned for you." Dale was a wonderful stepfather, and as usual, he drove cautiously and slowly. I had not seen the home they had purchased the year before and was excited to stay there. Mom worked one or two days a week as a nurse at a medical clinic, and Dale was a security guard at a group of condominiums. Greg was attending massage therapy school and living with them. Dale pulled into the garage that had a tennis ball hanging from the ceiling so he would know exactly where to stop. Greg brought in my luggage, and Mom took me to my room. Mom had baked some apple cobbler, and we caught up on news as we enjoyed time together. Slithering into bed, I was exhausted from the emotional week. The smell of freshly laundered sheets was calming. I thanked God until I finally closed my eyes for the night.

Waking up to the aroma of coffee and walking into the dining room where Mom was preparing fruit cups for us was pure joy. We drank coffee out of her teacups and saucers, and we talked for a few hours about a multitude of things. It was quite a memorable reunion for both of us. We watched *The 700 Club* together, enjoying every moment of being together.

Feeling compelled to at least check on the dates of the winter term at Evangel University, I discovered classes were starting for the winter term in five days. I prayed a prayer that included my surrendering to the Lord and my willingness to attend college if that was what He wanted. It is one of those prayers you pray when you're reasonably sure God won't ask you to do what you just agreed to. I made a call to the admissions office, and one of the staff helped me complete an application over the phone. Three hours later, Evangel called and approved my coming in the winter term. Mom and Dale did not have the financial resources to send me to college. I had no money and hadn't even taken the SAT exams.

It was early afternoon when the phone rang, and Mom said it was for me. Surprised someone was calling me, I took the phone. "Hello, Barbara. This is Lorraine Schwartz, the lady on the plane." "Oh yes, Lorraine." "I hope you don't mind, but I called The Walter Hoving Home and asked for your number. I'd like to visit you tomorrow. Are you available?" "Why certainly, Lorraine; what time would you like to come?" After confirming times and directions, Mom and I said how thrilled we were to have Lorraine visit all the way from Miami. "She's Jewish, so let's get some bagels, cream cheese, and lox," I suggested with exuberance. Mom agreed, and as we sat on the porch watching a radiant golden sunset, we prayed for Lorraine's visit.

"She just pulled up, Mom."

We opened the door and welcomed Lorraine with smiles and a big hug.

"Come in and have a seat." After Mom and Lorraine visited for a few moments, we gathered around an elegantly decorated table Mom had designed early that morning. Three kinds of bagels, strawberry, regular cream cheese, and fresh lox, were arranged in front of us. Lorraine shared about her life with her podiatrist husband, Irving, and a myriad of other topics women tend to gab about. I told her my application at Evangel had been accepted and I could come for the winter term. After an hour or so, Lorraine turned to me and said, "Barbara, I was so impressed with the story you shared on our plane ride; I just had to come and visit you." As she opened her purse, she continued, "You said you might be going to college, and Irving and I want to help you." She pulled out a check and handed it to me. It was the amount I needed to go to Missouri, where Evangel University was located. Lorraine continued, "As I hand this to you, Barbara, I say *L'chaim*! In Hebrew *L'chaim* means 'to good health' or 'to your well-being'!" Not expecting such sensitivity and generosity, I knew she was a special woman and I'd remain in contact with her. We exchanged contact information and hugged. Lorraine smiled as she got in her car and drove off.

The financial department agreed I could come without money upfront. Two days later, I was on the campus of Evangel University. I was assigned an academic advisor who directed me to humanity classes and a required Christianity 101 class. Not knowing what "humanity classes" meant, I signed up to take the minimal amount of credits. The next few weeks I spent adjusting to college life. I was thankful that I discovered Sodom and Gomorrah were cities and not sisters before I opened my mouth and displayed my ignorance. Feeling insecure and awkward, I avoided eye contact and social situations. Most of my time was spent studying, but gradually I got accustomed to life on campus.

I wrote to Lorraine regularly, telling her about my classes and the remarkable relationships I was developing. Evangel College became an incubator for my intellectual, emotional, and spiritual growth. Mom and Dale regularly sent what they could to cover textbooks and snacks.

In the second year, I declared biblical studies as my major and, in the second semester, received a thousand-dollar scholarship. My time was consumed with studying. Deep in my heart, I needed to prove that I had the intellectual capacity to learn and achieve in college. Driven by a compulsion to validate myself to others, I was consumed with studying. A seemingly huge barrier paralyzed me when I found out I needed to take Koine Greek to graduate as a biblical studies major. Not even sure what a prepositional phrase was, I wondered, *How can I take Greek when I don't even know English?* Sitting in my first Greek class, I noticed a dark-haired girl younger than me. We exchanged smiles, and I followed her out of class. "Hi, I'm Barb; what's your name?" "Hi, Barb. I'm Gail." Gail became my friend and my angel as we studied Greek together, and she helped me learn English by learning Greek.

The friendships I developed at Evangel and the challenges of each class led me deeper into a commitment to knowing the Scriptures.

In my mission became more evident that I wanted to lead others to the author of life by speaking the Word of God and loving people to Christ.

At age twenty-five I was one of the more mature freshmen. Older students typically lived off campus, but there were a few of us that opted for the dormitory life. "Why not ask Rick Gilliam out? He's about your age, and he's a biblical studies and history major," my biblical studies professor said. "No, I'd never ask a guy out, and I think he has a girlfriend," I responded. Picking up my books, I started to the library without another thought of Rick Gilliam or dating any man. With my shoulders back and determination in my step, I whispered to myself, *I don't need or want a man in my life; I've had enough. It's just You and me, Jesus.* I was reminded that there are no lone rangers in the kingdom of God. Being part of the community of faith is not an option. We are to live in an interdependent relationship with one another. The church is our home; though not perfect, we are the body of Christ.

Rick and I were friendly and shared a few classes together. We talked during lunch on occasion, and I found him engaging and fun. His dark hair and well-built stature added to his charm and appeal. Rick was quiet compared to the loud, showboat personality types I dated in the past. He started to pick me up for church, and we spent time together on campus.

Believing a kiss was the cork that opened the bottle leading to sex, I shielded myself and diligently kept a safe distance. Rick was patient and understanding, though he did not know my story. Sexuality was not a subject talked about in these Christian circles.

In the second year at Evangel University, I was contacted by the Assemblies of God for an interview describing the story of God's transformation in my life. An article was published two months later with my testimony from that interview. Within months I was contacted by John Benton, president of The Walter Hoving Home, to accompany him and another graduate from the program to the then-thriving and celebrated resort and television production campus of *The Jim and Tammy Show* in South Carolina. The facilities were elegant, and we were treated as stars. As we were called on stage for our interview with Jim Bakker, among other facts, he introduced me by saying, "This lady's brain was fried from drugs and alcohol, and now she's a straight-A student at Evangel College." Of course, the focus of such a miraculous event was the Lord Himself. Applause and worship electrified the air as the interview concluded.

The final year at Evangel was demanding and draining. I was exhausted, yet adrenaline flowed strongly at the probability of graduating with a three-point-nine grade point average. After four and a half years, I graduated summa cum laude. Two weeks before graduation, I stood at my mailbox and opened a note from the biblical studies department. Commonly assuming the worst, I was quick to open the note. "I'm receiving the outstanding philosophy award for the graduating class," I said out loud. It was unimaginable, and I danced and cried in my dorm room that day. Walking down the aisle on graduation day to receive my awards and diploma, I tried to maintain poise and appear as a confident scholastic graduate. Convinced everyone could hear my knees knocking, I took deep breaths and heard a still voice simply say, "Enjoy it." A sizable smile glimmered throughout the ceremony. I marinated for hours about each detail of the day and looked toward heaven and hollered to myself, "We did it, Lord." We had achieved As in all three years of Greek; we could now identify quartz and crystal after taking geology classes and learned how to write a thesis statement in English class. My family attended the ceremony and participated in all the receptions and festivities.

Tossing myself on my bed that night, I stared at the ceiling with a perpetual grin and promptly began reflecting on my life during my time at Evangel University from the day I stepped foot on the campus. The profound effect of the experiences filled me with gratitude and a sense of unbelief. It was my breeding ground of intellectual, emotional, relational, and spiritual growth. As I played with the tassels on my graduation regalia, I wiped away tears of thanksgiving, humbled by what the Lord had done. Mom knocked on my door and lay down next to me as we rested, knowing it was well with our souls. "If it wasn't for you, Mom, this would never have happened. You put me on every prayer list and ceased to give up on me even when it appeared hopeless. You loved me to Jesus." Reaching over to give her a mega hug, I said, "I love you, Mom; you are the best."

The life-changing relationships with faculty, staff, and students would continue years after graduation.

Graduating from Evangel University a year before Rick, I wasn't sure if I'd see him again.

Rick relocated to Mississippi after graduation to start a master's program in history. We called one another regularly, though our schedules were brimming with activities and challenges.

During the year I worked at the Home, I invited Lorraine and her husband to visit the Home, but only Lorraine was able to come. The hugs and the welcome from me and the other girls and staff would not soon be forgotten. I shared how I met Lorraine on the plane the day I left Walter Hoving Home and how she was instrumental in getting me to Missouri to college by paying for my airline ticket. Lorraine came for lunch, and after a tour, the ladies' choir sang a few songs in Lorraine's honor. It was a memorable reunion, and when Lorraine and I were alone, I shared the story of the Messiah, Jesus Christ, and what He did on the cross. After a time of questions and discussion, Lorraine made a decision to give her life to Christ and follow Him.

Months after leaving Evangel, I returned to New York and worked for The Walter Hoving Home, establishing a crisis center in the city for prostitutes and addicts. The work had an element of danger in offering a life off the streets for many of the women. The presence of pimps caused a high-risk situation for the addicts and prostitutes, as well as the people who offered them an alternative lifestyle off the streets. The New York City pimp squad patrolled the areas where prostitutes congregated and the pimps tended to avoid. Police surveillance made it safer to talk to the women.

"Hi, what's your name?" I asked one of the younger girls secluded under a bridgeway in the Lower East Side of Manhattan.

"I'm Rosie."

"Hey, Rosie, do you want to come in the mobile canteen and talk? We have fresh coffee and donuts." "Just bring me some coffee and a donut, and we can talk here."

As I filled up the Styrofoam cup with coffee and grabbed a vanilla donut, I surrendered the thin, young girl to the Lord.

"Here you are, Rosie. How long have you been out here?"

"Oh, about a year, but I'll get a better job sometime soon."

As the conversation progressed, Rosie told me this:

"Most girls give sex to men, but at least I get paid for it. I'm smarter than they are."

We spoke of a better life off the streets, and I invited her to leave tonight and go to The Walter Hoving Home with me. She said she wasn't ready to leave her life, but maybe soon. I gave her a card to The Walter Hoving Home, and we drove up to Times Square. The Salvation Army shared resources with us and offered to share their office in Times Square for services and counseling.

The year went by quickly, and a desire to further my theological education deepened. I visited my choice of seminaries outside of Boston. Gordon-Conwell Theological Seminary had one of the finest and most prestigious reputations in the country. The work would be strenuous because the Boston area is a place of academia plus. Gordon-Conwell alone had several noted Bible scholars on faculty; one in particular, Dr. Gordon D. Fee, was a New Testament scholar affiliated with the Assemblies of God.

I enrolled at Gordon-Conwell Theological Seminary in the fall of 1983 and lived in a house with six other women. Anticipating learning Hebrew and sitting under the teaching of Dr. Gordon Fee and others, I adjusted quickly. Classes called for rigorous study and my complete attention. Feeling proud to be at Gordon-Conwell, I started looking forward to developing meaningful relationships and getting acquainted with the various ministries in Boston. Because of the multitude of seminaries and universities in Boston, a consortium between the educational institutions existed. A Catholic philosopher and priest, Dr. Henri Nouwen was a noted author and speaker. He taught a class at Harvard Divinity School on spirituality, and I was not going to miss it.

Eager to get to the class early, I left Gordon-Conwell at 7 a.m. to drive the twenty-eight miles to Cambridge. Finding the classroom at Harvard Divinity school, I sat in the second row so I'd be close to Dr. Nouwen. The seats were fixed and arranged in an auditorium style. His class on spirituality was unique in using imagery and blending in of psychology and philosophy. Dr. Nouwen focused on the importance of going from the house of fear to the house of intimacy. After the intensity of learning Greek and the details of New Testament Survey, the simplicity of using the image of two houses of fear and faith was compelling.

I spent a summer in between semesters in 1984 in New York City, working with a team to locate lost and exploited children being trafficked. When I described the sale and abuse of the children, we encountered many found it unthinkable and did not believe the truth. The trafficking of children and women has progressed so rapidly and extensively that the world lacks trained people to work with this population.

I was unprepared for the evil of disrobed teenage girls dancing in triple X shops, open prostitution, and a club full of people doing sadomasochistic acts; it was overwhelming and oppressive. I was part of a team that went undercover for the FBI, as it was known they were selling children. Describing what I saw would be received with skepticism, especially in the religious community. My soul and mind felt contaminated, and the longer I stayed in New York City, the more distressed and alarmed I became. Returning to Gordon-Conwell and being immersed in studying and in ministry, I failed to give myself time to process what I had experienced. Fatigue and depression covertly began to penetrate my body and mind. I ignored the shout of my soul to stop running and be still so God could speak to me. Oblivious and deaf to my own pain, I hid behind academics and the need to help others. After all it is much easier to pull the sliver out of someone else than to recognize and have the sliver taken out of my own self. I began to decline in physical stamina and felt mentally foggy much of the time and less hopeful or spiritual. My motivation decreased, and I felt depressed. Questioning why I would be depressed took some exploring and waiting.

A couple of weeks later, I had a vision/dream that God tapped me on the shoulder and said, "Barbara, there are things in your life that you and I need to consider." Without stopping what I was doing in the vision, I said, "But, God, I'm busy for You. I'm building a ministry, and some people want me to share on Christian television."

So the Lord turned out the lights, and I fell into a deep depression in the following weeks. It was challenging to just get out of bed and attend class. "Set an appointment with this doctor, and he can help you," the nurse at the seminary said as she handed me his card.

It was as though God had put a muzzle on me long enough to sit still and listen to Him. Wounds from past abuse needed to be acknowledged and felt, along with poor self-worth and other baggage from a life of sin and deception. He used His Word and the Holy Spirit to prod and tap some harbored wounds that drained my energy and ability to be free. "Stop hiding behind, Barbara, and using loads of God language to avoid your own pain. I love you more than you'll ever know, and I don't care if you never do another thing in My name; you require My healing and time spent wrapped in My unconditional love before you can move forward.

"You cannot pay Me back nor impress Me with your education or abilities. I gave it all to you." I was convinced God's love had no agenda but to make me healthy. A picture of a young, bruised, and fractured girl hiding behind the ultimate parent, God, peeking out and mimicking what the parent said flashed in my mind. God launched a process that was my dark night of the soul. Symptoms of clinical depression increased as I begged God to turn the lights on again. The light of the world, full of grace and truth, was present with every breath, but I could not see or understand. I developed anorexia and bulimia as a means of controlling something that was so foreign and painful. But control is only an illusion for humans. The changes in my conversation and behavior were obvious to friends and professors. I began to see my medical doctor for treatment. He was also a therapist and agreed to see me. The metamorphosis began, and no matter how hard I worked to kick a hole in the chrysalis and escape, Jesus held me tightly. Months passed as the Lord worked His miracle of exposing my pain and the secrets that kept me from soaring.

The worn-out recording of lies that played repeatedly in my mind impacted my life choices and self-perception. Lies that pounded my mind and said I was not capable or suitable for success and should live with what I could grab in life. Lies popped up their ugly head and said God was not good and could never forgive me or that a decent man would not want to marry me. All were self-defeating thoughts that drove out all hope for a future life. God's promises made new recordings that would catapult me into a new life of purpose and opportunity.

It is not an easy road to change and to feel years of comfortable, though faulty and destructive, ways of thinking to be transformed. This process required that I recognize and admit the presence and power of deceptive and destructive thinking and beliefs. As in numerous changes necessary throughout life, surrendering old and decayed thinking is not as easy as it may seem. A certain comfort level of thought that justifies how a person's life gets overturned and replaced by truth is like getting used to a new set of teeth or being able to hear. During the very difficult days when I felt such shame and defeat, I stood on the Word of God. Many times I meditated on passages like the last verse of Psalm 23, verse 6 (NIV), "Surely your goodness and love will follow me all the days of my life, and I will dwell in the house of the Lord forever." Or Psalm 54:4 (NIV), "Surely God is my help; the Lord is the one who sustains me."

During this time of uncertainty and distress, fellow students and professors surrounded me like angels present around the gates of heaven. "Are not all angels ministering spirit sent to serve those who will inherit salvation?" Hebrews 1:14, (NIV).

"The angel of the LORD encamps all around those who fear Him and delivers them" Psalm 34:7, (NIV).

Dr. Gordon Fee and his wife, Maudine, observed the seriousness of my depression and invited me to live off-campus with them until I could heal. Dr. Gordon Fee is one of the leading New Testament scholars in the world and is one of the central reasons I choose Gordon-Conwell Theological Seminary. He is Pentecostal and is affiliated with the Assemblies of God, teaching and ministering globally.

"But you're Gordon Fee; I'm not anyone special. I'm no one."

"Oh yes, you are," Dr. Fee responded. "Jesus is the great equalizer, and our worth is the same to Him."

The Fees lived near the seminary, and I could walk if necessary. Hesitantly I moved in with them after we agreed to a few arrangements.

Because I was losing more weight in my battle with anorexia and bulimia, I had to be home for family dinners and not vomit the contents of the meal. Dr. Fee made my breakfast and, on occasion, washed my car.

As Dr. Fee set a plate of scrambled eggs, toast, and bacon in front of me one morning, he said:

"The most spiritual thing you can do, Barbara, is to eat. I don't understand all the emotional dynamics occurring, but losing more weight could be dangerous."

A well-known professor of church history, Dr. Richard Lovelace, offered prayers for me with compassion and sensitivity. This was the church in action at its best.

My experiences at Evangel and Gordon-Conwell reminded me of when Jesus called His friend Lazarus from the tomb of death, where he had lain for four days. After four days in that crypt, Jesus simply cried out, "Lazarus, come out," in front of His sisters and others (John 11:43). At once the dead man came and was bound in his hands with stripes of linen and a cloth around his face. Then Jesus instructed those around Lazarus to take off the stinky, dirty grave clothes so he could move forward. Jesus could have done it, but He employed His followers to participate in Lazarus' complete restoration. That is what Gordon Fee and his wife and many more did for me. After Jesus called me forth from the darkness of the tomb of death, He asked others to help me move forward by removing my smelling and filthy clothes or hurts and wounds that kept me from moving ahead (John 11:38–44). Living with the Fee family was a sizeable part of reframing my perceptions about myself and the world according to God's truth. Gathering around the table with family and breaking bread together created a sense of belonging. Engaged in honest communication around the dinner table and being present for one another was life-altering. A deeper understanding and love for how the church functions were modeled to me in a variety of ways.

Though a slow process, it was a pivotal time of healing and cultivating a new aspect of my relationship with the Lord.

A particular truth about Jesus' death on the cross struck me with such depth and reality. The Holy Spirit brought deeper freedom and understanding of what it meant to be declared righteous. It's a legal term used in the Bible to describe the act of God in which He declares that a person is not guilty. A justified person is in a state of full acceptance with God.

A Roman Catholic monk by the name of Martin Luther was best known for the phrase "Justification by faith." He was constantly striving desperately to find a sense of acceptance with God by going to confession, sometimes numerous times daily. The realization and power of living as a person justified by faith in Christ and not adherence to the law freed Luther forever.

It was during this time that Luther's best-noted phrase and understanding of faith entered my soul and mind like a jolt of life-saving medicine. "Justification by faith" became my motto and war cry. Paul, the apostle, writes in numerous scriptures in the book of Romans about the supreme liberation from the law and of our freedom in Christ and acceptance of what He did for us on the cross.

He is more concerned about my being than my doing. If I never do another task in ministry or produce good grades, God cannot love me any more or less. It is such a counterintuitive truth in our culture that thrives on achieving and producing. For more than a year, I battled clinical depression, ultimately agreeing to take a low-dose antidepressant. Feeling vulnerable and emotionally and spiritually frail, I allowed the sovereign and gentle hand of God to undertake to remove a vast amount of inner wreckage and pain that had accumulated over several years. A toxic infection that was oozing with poison kept me sick in my soul. No amount of bandages worked at this stage, and shame took a backseat to healing. Oblivious that I would fall in love and eventually marry, the dark night of agonizing paralyzing depression prepared me for marriage with a wonderful man. Rick and I met at Evangel, and our union was a gift from the Lord.

In April of 1985, Rick came to Boston to visit, and four months later, we were married.

Marriage is an adjustment that requires mutual communication and respect and self-awareness of our personal experiences that impact our perspective and beliefs about self, others, and God. Developmental influences and experiences growing up impact our perspective of marriage and relationships.

I continued to recover from clinical depression, and periods of intense stress exaggerated my symptoms. Graduating from seminary with a master's in religious education included a course in internal transformation that was not in the syllabus but was a unique, specific experience only the Holy Spirit could accomplish. Could it be that more seminaries should consider making space for these encounters with the Lord to more adequately prepare pastors? Call it inner healing or deliverance—God attended to my hidden internal brokenness and began to disinfect and mend me. In the midst of a number of expert theologians, I had a class with the one who wrote the book, the all-perfect and powerful professor. The recovery was a process that brightened the light of the truth of God's unconditional love and grace that frees a person from working to attain His love and approval. Had God not allowed issues behind my depression to come to the surface and be addressed, I do not believe I would have gotten married.

During the first year of marriage, I often woke up saying, "Rick is too good to be true; I know I'll come home one day and he'll be gone." Self-talk included, *I'm not a great cook like Rick's family; wonder if I cannot bear children. Can I meet up to his standards for cleanliness?* It is labor-intensive for me to stay organized in my closet and to focus on household duties. Rick knew I wasn't the typical, stereotypical woman who would spend hours preparing gourmet food. He believed I was called to full-time ministry, so he helped at home, and his expectations were balanced.

In the midst of these adjustments, Rick and I were presented with job opportunities in Southern California. His mother and uncle were living in the same county where our employment was located. Unaware of how my unconscious mind would influence my behavior, I began to sabotage our relationship by pushing Rick away. Fear roared its ugly voice again, feeding me lies I had to dismiss with the Word of God. Catching diseases like cancer early and eliminating them is critical for a positive prognosis. The quicker unjustified fear is recognized and wiped out, the healthier we become. Sensing my insecurity, Rick one afternoon gently put his hands on my shoulders, looked me straight in the eyes, and said, "Barbara, I'm committed to you until death do us part." "Oh, you are. Okay," I swiftly responded. It was as though the truth that Rick loved me dazzled me as never before. It seeped into my mind and heart like a tea strainer allowing only quality tea to fill the cup. Able to accept what Rick said, I knew that he was not the source of my happiness, nor could I expect to him to make me happy. Even though I was joyfully anticipating a multitude of happy times with him, God remained the source of provision and joy.

Not accepting your spouse as he or she is and not letting go of silent expectations for the person to change and believing you can change the person is a setup for problems. Releasing the need to feel in control brings acceptance and peace. Living with expectancy in God and praying for our spouse make space to adjust. Although I fail at practicing this principle, I can live in anticipation and adaptability, which provides me with a greater ability to enjoy life with my husband as our love grows. Amending our expectations of others and of ourselves can awaken any relationship. Celebrating all that has been and continues to be forgiven in my life is a stark reminder of my need to forgive others. Forgiving self can be most difficult but renders the ability to move forward, not spending frivolous energy and resources falling backward.

Acknowledging what is uncomfortable is like a pebble in our shoes, yet it meets a need in our life that we find difficult to let go of. Even resentment can provide a justification for behavior that helps us remain a victim and live in self-pity. Self-awareness is essential in understanding why and how we can act in unhealthy ways that eventually damage our relationships and our freedom to serve the Lord. There is a saying around people in recovery that says, "Holding onto resentment is like drinking poison hoping it affects the other person."

Ten years later, Rick and I were living in Southern California, and I was working as a therapist and pastor at a chemical dependency hospital. Also pursuing my second master's degree in counseling. I became familiar with family systems and the various roles family members play. Family systems therapy centers on the family as a whole unit. The approach suggests that the family is more than the sum of its parts, and each person is part of an emotional connection. In families where alcoholism and drug addiction are present, the system loses a sense of homeostasis or stability between the members. Feeling disconnected from family occurs when trauma or secret rules are experienced but not discussed. There is a saying that states a family is as "sick as its secrets." Claudia Black said in her online education video "It Will Never Happen to Me" that alcoholic and dysfunctional families follow three unspoken rules:

1. Don't talk. We don't talk about our family problems to each other or to outsiders.
2. Don't trust. Children depend on their parents or caregivers to keep them safe, but when you grow up in a dysfunctional family, you don't experience your parents (and the world) as safe and nurturing.

3. Don't feel. Repressing painful or confusing emotions is a coping strategy used by everyone in a dysfunctional family. Children in dysfunctional families witness their parents numbing their feelings with alcohol, drugs, food, pornography, and technology. Rarely are feelings expressed and dealt with in a healthy way.[x]

Insight: What family secrets kept you from being honest about who you are?

Chapter 8:

Me, a Pastor?

The following years opened new opportunities working as a hospice chaplain, a substance abuse counselor, and speaking at numerous women's events. One day I received a call from my elderly minister friend. "Hi, Barbara. This is Marguerite; Roy is sick, and I'm scheduled to speak at a storefront church in North Long Beach this coming Sunday. Could you substitute for me? The church is not in the best section of Long Beach; it's located between a furniture store and a liquor store two doors down. Many years ago, I attended there, and I was filled with the Holy Spirit; it was a lively church with great worship." "Sure, Marguerite, anything for you and Roy." I arrived that Sunday and parked on the street near a funeral home. The building had a small marque on the stucco left side saying "North Long Beach Tabernacle" in black letters. I opened the door and walked on the worn-out dark blue carpet. Wood paneling throughout the church with pictures of churches the small congregation had planted in their fifty-six years lined the entrance hall. Later I discovered the caring congregation had started 166 churches worldwide. It was clean but old. The congregation consisted of older White people, Filipino families, and a few African American folks. The seats were old movie theater chairs reupholstered in maroon leather. The service went well, and the people were welcoming and loving. They asked if I'd come back in a couple of weeks, informing me that their Filipino pastor had died several months earlier.

After parking in the driveway, I darted into the house and set my purse and Bible down as I headed to the bedroom, where Rick was lying downing watching baseball.

"The people are wonderful, and they invited me back. The congregation is searching for a pastor, as their minister died a couple of months ago," I blurted out.

Rick looked up and said, "You should apply to be the pastor, honey."

"They wouldn't vote in a female pastor after fifty-six years of all-male leadership," I replied.

"Do it anyway."

Later that week, I spoke to the network superintendent in charge of all the churches in our area about North Long Beach Tabernacle.

"Barb," he said while shaking his head, "we've had people try out, but no one wants to raise their family in that area; it's become a dangerous neighborhood."

"Then that's the place for me." I smiled in response.

"Great, Barb. We'd love to have you there."

The government of the church is set up so the congregation votes in or out the pastor.

I spoke to Eleanor Schaffer, the woman designated to lead the search in finding a new pastor. That week it was set for me to preach the following Sunday again and for Rick and me to attend a little gathering after in the back.

"Lord, I recall as I was being sentenced by the court to the girl's reformatory, I promised I'd never set foot in a church again. Now, I am actually applying to pastor a church. God, You know I may have had Greek and Hebrew, but I still don't know phonics or how to pronounce those complex names of people and cities in the Bible. Maybe if I say them quickly, no one will know the difference." The following couple of weeks, I spent time getting to know the people who called North Long Beach Tabernacle their church home. In October of 1997, I was voted pastor of the church. That week I asked, "What do I do now, Lord?" His profound wisdom still stands as it did then. "Love the people, Barbara, and preach the truth."

Because this was a small, multicultural congregation, it took time for me to understand and accept that punctuality was not always part of the practices, especially for the various cultures. They valued relationships over being consistently prompt. I adapted because I witnessed all the people, mostly their relatives, they had to go pick up and bring to church. Aware of my WASP (White, Anglo-Saxon, Protestant) philosophy, which included a strong work ethic and believing it was a Christian value, I soon moved it down my list of priorities.

The family-like environment was warm and caring. Most of these folks were down-to-earth, honest people who had worked hard all their lives. They cared deeply about their church and their community. Some walked to church or took the bus, and another man hosed down the alcove to the door due to the stench of urine before picking up his family for church. In the back of the sanctuary were tambourines used during worship that were made of pop-bottle caps. Most of the carbonated beverages they came from were not on the market any longer. The church was filled with history, which was written in various logs through the years.

Among the precious people of this church was an older couple named Eleanor and Paul Schaeffer. They had been part of this church since its inception and were wonderful leaders. Everyone called them "Pop" and "Nanny." Nanny was a plain-looking woman with shoulder-length gray hair. She always had a rhinestone Jesus pin on her dress and a crocheted cross around her neck, and her smile was angelic. The informal worship services took some getting used to for me, but their love for God and one another was obvious. Nanny had a habit of praying every time she heard a siren. One Sunday morning, while I was preaching, I saw Nanny quietly bow her head and begin praying silently as sirens were rushing past the church. A few weeks later, I heard her teaching the seven-year-olds in Sunday school; she was teaching them how to pray when they heard sirens. "The men and women answering the call in that vehicle need our prayers for protection and strength. Make sure to pray for their families too. It's not easy being a policeman, fireman, or paramedic. The person who needs the emergency service needs our continued prayers too. Your prayers make a difference; even if you don't know the people, God does!" I found myself becoming more mindful when I heard a siren, even starting to follow Nanny's example.

The following story tells of one of many miraculous times God intervened. The value of learning from others in the church leaves an eternal stamp, especially when you are the pastor.

One Sunday evening, the church attended a special regional service in the convention center in Anaheim. I was part of the prayer team for that event, so I did not sit with my church. Spending time with people who came forward for prayer, I left after most people were gone. As I was driving home, I noticed two police cars and an ambulance on the corner.

Lights were flashing, and part of the road was closed off. Almost automatically I began to pray for everyone involved in this emergency. The entire way driving home, I prayed, "Lord, whoever has the emergency, protect and heal them. Get them the help they need quickly, and comfort and strengthen the families." Nanny's words rang in my head, "You may not know them, but God does, and they need our prayers." I fell asleep quickly that night, feeling good about the service. At about 6:30 a.m., the phone rang; barely reaching the call on time, I answered.

"Pastor Barbara?"

"Yes," I replied. I didn't recognize the voice.

"This is Paul Schaeffer; I'm at the intensive care unit at Anaheim Memorial. Nanny had a heart attack while driving last night, right after we left the convention center. Something told me to grab the wheel like I knew exactly what to do so that we avoided an accident." I quickly got up and began to get ready to go to the hospital. At once I was struck by the realization that the emergency vehicles and the flashing lights last night on my way home were for Nanny. She was the recipient of my prayers that she modeled throughout the years for everyone needing emergency services.

Nanny's faithfulness and example came back to save her during her life-threatening crisis.

When I arrived at the intensive care unit, Pop greeted me with eyes filled with tears. I was told by medical staff she was in serious condition, so I cautiously approached her bedside, and a nurse informed me she could not hear me or know I was there. I doubted the nurse's evaluation as I prayed silently. The prayer team was notified before I left the house, so I knew many were lifting up Nanny before the throne of God. I held Nanny's hand and spent time in the waiting room with the family. Later that afternoon, I sat next to Nanny's bed, made eye contact with her, and whispered in her ear:

"Nanny, do you know I am?"

Though an oxygen mask obscured her talking, she looked directly into my eyes and said:

"Sure, I do. You're Pastor Barbara."

"What church do you go to, Nanny?"

"North Long Beach Tabernacle," she replied.

I smiled as my eyes welled up with tears. She was going to be okay. After quadruple bypass surgery, Nanny made a full recovery and lived another ten years. She still prayed every time she heard a siren, but for all of us, it was more than a ritual; it was a personal testimony of one woman's caring example of answered prayer. Eleanor Schaeffer reaped the care and prayers she had sown into many lives, including mine.

Years later, Nanny was told she had macular degeneration. It wasn't at a critical stage, and she continued to drive. Her husband, Paul, preferred her to drive for reasons unknown. Nanny was one of the most cheerful, godly women I have ever met. Never did I hear her speak a rumor or gossip about another person. A year or more after Nanny's diagnosis, I noticed she was straining to see. I asked if she should still be driving, and I shall never forget her answer. With an enthusiastic grin and self-confidence in her voice, she replied:

"Oh sure, Pop tells me when the light turns yellow." A short time later, Nanny had to quit driving, but there was no shortage of people who cherished picking her up for church. As years passed like an arrow from a bow, Nanny and Pop's health declined. When I visited Nanny at her home one day, she said:

"I'm praying Pop and I die at about the same time."

With barely a muster seed of faith and a barrel full of doubt, I thought, *That probably won't happen.*

Oh, me of little faith.

Months later, Paul and Eleanor Schaeffer died within three days of each other. One of the unsurpassed gifts I received in ministry was to officiate at a joint funeral celebration for both Eleanor and Paul Schaeffer. Paul and Eleanor's daughter, Sherry, continued to oversee a church this couple planted in South Africa. The church had grown, and the believers were a significant part of the community.

The gravity of needs and challenges inside the church and in the community were unimaginable at times. Reasonable boundaries are essential for church leaders, especially when a leader swallows the expectation that the pastor should care for all who come to him or her for help. It is then effortless to fall into performing for the approval of others, which becomes unending and can lead to burnout and other health problems. After the pastor has bought into that myth, marriages and family life can suffer also.

All human beings, but especially Christians, must remember to maintain a sense of humor. Humanity should never cease to amaze us. Someone said having a daily laugh is like inner jogging. Perhaps age has brought me to a realization that life is too short to take myself too seriously.

On another occasion, a man named Al and his family were an intricate part of our church family. He stood up at a Sunday night service to give a testimony of how God saved his life the previous week. Al worked as a security guard at the local branch of a large bank. Tuesday, around 2:00 p.m., three men entered the bank with scarves around their nose and mouth. They yelled for everyone to get on the floor while taking Al's gun and said to him:

"You're coming with us."

Fleeing the scene, they shoved Al in the back seat of a 1998 red Grand Prix and sped off. Al said he told them he had a family and he just wanted to go home to them. Being the sole breadwinner, Al pleaded to let him go. Dead silence filled the sanctuary as Al continued.

Al described the guy holding a gun to his head as in his mid-forties. Al said he continued talking.

"I'm involved with my church and a strong Christian," Al continued.

The man holding the gun to said with an eager and joyful voice: "Oh wow, I'm a Christian too."

They dropped Al off at the next corner. Thankful Al was un-harmed, I sighed and thought to myself, *I would never have fathomed that ending.*

Though a tense and dangerous encounter, I chuckled later at the response of the man holding the gun that he, too, was a Christian.

On several occasions while driving into the church parking lot, I said out loud, "Do I really have the privilege of being the pastor to these diverse and amazing people?" Pews filled with a variety of ethnic and socio-economic worshippers who loved the Lord felt like a blessing I did not deserve.

The Silent Retreat That Started Me Talking

Two years into pastoring the storefront church, I was approached by a larger Assemblies of God Church less than two miles away. The pastor's wife had seen an article I had written in the local Long Beach paper and proposed a possible merger. After lengthy dialog with the board, we voted unanimously to pursue a potential merger with the larger church. The beautiful church sat on a strategic corner in North Long Beach.

The pastor's health and the health of the church had been declining over a twenty-year period. He suffered from dementia and other health problems. The leadership appeared indifferent to the extreme transitions in the neighborhood and in the congregation. Every organization experiences life cycles, and intervention before it becomes critical is pivotal if the organization is to survive. Signs of approaching death were present in every aspect of the church, and they were barely breathing. From a near-empty bank account to an empty church, the board was too elderly and too tired to take action. Though the community had transitioned into a low-income, multicultural neighborhood, the congregation was comprised of mostly older Caucasian members who remained in the church but no longer lived in the neighborhood. Hoping to return to times past when the Spirit moved as they remembered, one by one they slowly died and went home to heaven. There was no returning to the good old days, and unless relief came soon, the church would close. The sad reality was that if the church closed, the community would not have noticed.

The merger was finalized a few months later, and we moved the small storefront people to the church named Glad Tidings. Naïve about the serious condition of the church's hidden problems of hiring family members, not paying the secretaries' retirement, and other secrets, we faced each problem as it appeared and worked toward solutions. After a few years of striving to restart this lifeless congregation and attract new people, I questioned my leadership abilities to build the church. Many of the seniors were dying, and I was doing more funerals than outreach. Although I loved pastoring these wonderful men and women and facilitating their memorial services, the decline in attendance was troubling for me.

I was part of a group of Assembly of God pastors in my geographical area. We met on a monthly basis for fellowship and on occasion to be informed about forthcoming events. Being one of the few female senior pastors in the network, I felt slightly obligated to attend. Though most pastors denied competing with one another, seldom did a meeting conclude without being asked what numbers we were running on Sunday morning. Growth and numbers were rewarded by leadership with speaking at events on church growth and a sign of healthy influence and management by the pastor. Because of the dwindling numbers of people due to death, I plotted to escape the gathering without being asked. Inevitably I was cornered by a group of pastors still sipping coffee who greeted me cordially and then asked the pressing question of what were my numbers in attendance on Sunday morning. Feeling compelled to share in the conversation, I thought about what to say. An attitude of nonconformity and protest filled my mind as I smiled to myself. "Oh, people are dropping like flies in my church. If you have any deacons you want to get rid of, call me, and I'll pray for them, and they will probably be in heaven in a short time. Sometimes I feel like Pastor Kevorkian." No one knew whether to laugh or say anything. I had become frustrated with the pressure to be successful but smiled as we chuckled together. With the same mindset of competition and definition of accomplishment as the pastors asking about my numbers, I understood my sarcasm and motivation needed to be realigned, and my response was probably not that funny to the Lord.

Times of reflection about the sometimes-humorous incidents provided occasional bursts of laughter. Lupe, the resident administrative assistant, had a stroke and lost her peripheral vision, and that was not funny. She longed to return to work after rehabilitation, and with the approval of doctors and her family, Lupe returned part time. Her husband, Robert, was the church custodian and was able to drive her to work. Robert was loyal to the church and a retired insurance salesman; they lived only a few miles from the church. Robert was at least 85 percent deaf and loved worshipping the Lord. He was on the worship team. Tears surged from his eyes each time he sang about Jesus. Unlocking my office door one morning, I saw Robert was on a ladder changing a light bulb while Lupe held the ladder in place.

"I need a different bulb, Lupe; can you go get me one in the closet?"

"What size do you need?"

"What? I can't hear you, Lupe."

"I'm in the closet; what size do you need?"

Lupe blaringly shouted. Staring at the light socket, Robert shouted:

"I still can't hear you, honey."

"Well, I can't see any larger bulbs, Robert."

I rushed to the closet to help Lupe find the correct bulb. Eventually the bulb got changed, and we went on with the day. But that would not be the last time Lupe's sight and Robert's hearing disabilities created delays. Looking toward the heavens, I said, "We are quite the motley crew You have here, God, myself included."

Though the people were wonderful, the challenges and responsibilities became overwhelming. Rick's company was not growing and succeeding as projected, and I felt weary and discouraged. One day with tears accumulating on my cheeks, I shouted, "I can't do this anymore, Lord!" I was depressed, burned out, and lonely. The stress was felt physically in increased blood pressure and painful neck strain. I didn't want to go home, and I didn't want to go to church.

Desperate to get alone and pray, I found a convent a few miles from my home where I could go for a one-person silent retreat. I needed the Lord and desperately longed to hear from Him. I checked in to the local convent on a Sunday afternoon when most weekend retreats had ended. I had the second floor of the retreat center to myself. My room at the end of the hall was simple but comfortable. It overlooked a colorful and well-groomed prayer garden. After settling in, I sighed deeply and, for the next few hours, detoxed from the noise of life. Quieting my heart and mind was more difficult than I anticipated. I woke up in the middle of the night feeling powerless, but the hushed sounds of crickets and trees in the wind served as a lullaby. The retreat center was close to the railroad tracks and the distant sound of a train during the night was soothing. The next morning, coffee and fruit were available to those on retreat, so after a tall coffee and chilled fruit, I settled into an overstuffed chair in the retreat library and read excerpts from a variety of resources. I focused on Matthew 11:29 (NIV) in several translations, "Take my yoke upon you and learn from me, for I am gentle and humble in heart, and you will find rest for your souls." I let the passage permeate my soul. As I put down my pen and closed my journal, I recognized the sun shining through a window and thought I'd top off the morning with a walk. The sun was bright, tempered by a gentle breeze. A walk in the prayer garden was invigorating and peaceful. Unusual but welcomed, I found myself dozing off in the afternoon.

On my final day at the retreat center, I woke up depressed and disappointed that God had not decisively spoken to me. How could I leave with no answers? I decided to spend the remainder of my time in the chapel. With my Bible in hand, I closed the door and knelt at a padded alter facing a small stained-glass design. I began to worship the Lord, and after what seemed like hours, I felt a strong sense of divine presence like I'd never experienced before. Captivated by the closeness of God, I pleaded with Him for direction and wisdom in leading the church. Calmly Jesus asked me why I didn't spend more time with Him. Unprepared for the question, I had no answer. What do I say to God, who knows a word before I speak it? Continuing to worship, I felt Jesus reach forward and place a triple-braided gold rope around my neck that instantly melted into my body like newly formed customized skin. He said, "This is your anointing; everyone has their own anointing." Sobbing and immobilized by the moment, I managed to stammer, "For me, just for me?" "Barbara, if you just follow Me, you'll know exactly what to do." At once I saw a road, and on each side of the road were hands lined up. Some of the hands were clapping, and some were praying. The Lord explained, "These are the people I put in your life to encourage you and to pray for you, and you are the hands of encouragement and prayer for others on their journey."

"But why do I feel stuck, unable to move forward?"

"You cannot advance because you are carrying yokes and burdens that are not yours to bear. Would you like to give them to Me?"

As Jesus spoke, I felt a bulky weight on my shoulders as though I had oversized mental rings around my neck and shoulders. Jesus named the yokes that were holding me down and restricting my movement. Included were the church finances, fear of being perceived as a poor leader, self-sufficiency, insecurity, and loneliness. Carefully removing the weights from my neck one at a time, I handed them to him.

"You have one more, Barbara; you continue to feel shame and responsibility for your father's sexual abuse when you were a little girl. It is not your yoke or burden to carry; it is his."

Shocked by His words, I slowly pulled the last weight from my shoulders and handed it to Jesus. Then I sensed Him reach deep in my soul to touch the edges where remnants of shame resided. Then the Lord requested the most astounding thing—to go and celebrate rejoicing in the God who restores dignity and lavishes us with love and understanding. That experience was the beginning of a transformational process that would affect every area of my life. As I started to stand up, I realized the anxiety and discouragement I had entered the room with were gone. Hours later, I became aware that I could move my neck from side to side with little to no pain. The crushing load that weighed me down had been removed. That night I replayed the experience multiple times, visualizing each moment and hanging onto every word. I came to the retreat to get answers, blinded to the fact I didn't even know the questions. Congregational life slowly started to improve as one of the Bible schools where I taught sent a team of student volunteers to help us on Sunday mornings. I was less anxious and had resolved to replace being driven to succeed so I appeared successful to peers and those in leadership to being guided by God's Holy Spirit. When I surrendered my expectations and moved out of the way, the Lord began to send a team of volunteers from a local Bible school where I taught. The team took responsibility for worship, children's church, and some administrative duties. There was more time for me to focus on building relationships with potential leaders and families and networking in the community. Acceptance of my limitations, coupled with a greater understanding of what God expected of me, resulted in a healthier balance and relationships.

Replaying the removal of the yoke of Dad's sexual abuse gnawed at me. The truth and the memories associated with the despicable acts crashed upon me in waves of shame and sorrow. I still had bouts of excusing his behavior because of his alcoholism and the consistent actions of the family to rescue and enable his reckless behavior. Overwhelmed by the thoughts and feelings, I managed to put the entire issue in a box and shove it to the back of my mind, or so I thought. Over a year later, I was advised by my physician to seek counseling due to increased blood pressure, headaches, and stomach problems. It was a year filled with stressful changes like the sudden death of a couple of church leaders, the retirement of the custodian, and the declining health of my administrative assistant. Avoiding seeing a therapist lasted for a few months, but I knew I could not continue to work longer and harder to compensate for the void left by those no longer able to serve. I recalled a sign I had seen that said, "Lord, help me bury my pride before my pride buries me." Finally, I picked up the phone and made an appointment with one of three referrals for counseling given by my insurance. An appointment was made for the following week. I was thankful the day I went that the waiting room was empty. After a few minutes, a tall, unassuming female therapist greeted me in the waiting room; smiling, she introduced herself and walked me into her office. Her office was small but warm and welcoming. While sitting in a large leather chair, I took a deep breath and tried to get comfortable in a pillow-filled loveseat.

Feeling less stressed after discovering she was a leader in the Lutheran Church and had worked with several pastors on the verge of burnout, I leaned back and felt my body relax.

"How can I help you, Barbara?" A sudden jolt of fear struck me as I took a deep breath.

"Well, a little too much stress is why I'm here."

We talked about my history and what led up to my present pastoral role. We agreed to meet again the following week when I described in greater detail the sources of stress. She gave me practical ways to manage the demands and set realistic boundaries. I had substituted being driven by my own definition of success and leadership for being guided by the Holy Spirit. Desiring to please the governing leadership and the congregation, I allowed pride and fear to camouflage my weariness and discouragement. All Father God desires for me and for you is to be His daughter or son; everything else is an outflow of that. Resting in God's love without guilt or condemnation takes faith and considerable trust. It is a lifetime in the making.

Lessons from a Rescue Dog

Stretched out on my office floor, my rescue dog Tabitha lay beside me, and her big brown eyes begged, "Scratch my tummy." Smiling, I obeyed and reached out my hand. "You suffered so much in your life. I'm glad we adopted you two years ago," The last of our three bichons had died six months earlier, and I was ready to adopt a new family member with a tail and four legs. Looking on rescue websites, I landed on one for bichon frise and poodle mixes. I completed an application in the hopes I would find a dog I wanted to meet. The following day I received a call.

"Hello, is this Barbara Gilliam? This is Marji with bichon rescue, where you put in an application." That call evolved to my agreeing to be a foster parent to a four- to five-year-old bichon who was a complete mess. The dog was at a nearby veterinarian hospital, where the doctor donated his time to certain rescue dogs. After approval to foster the dog, the vet called me.

"Hello, this is Dr. Meyer, and I understand you are interested in fostering and possibly adopting this dog. Well, she has a 25 or 30 percent chance of living. Her uterus is torn, and parts of puppies remain inside that are strangling her organs; we had to shave her hair and treat her with cream, for her paws were swollen. I'm astonished she is not writhing in pain. She still wages her tail and walks and acts as though she wants to play. I believe it depends on her will to survive and her strength. If she lives, she will defy a medical prognosis. I heard you're a pastor. Well, we've done everything medical science can do, so you better pray. It depends on her strength and her will to live. Call me at eleven tomorrow for an update."

Though I hadn't met her, I began to cry and prayed for her. I cried out to the Lord that night, "God, if she lives, I'll share her story to encourage women who have been abused and degraded to be strong and rise above the odds." I summoned people all over the country to pray for her. At 11 a.m. the next day, I took a deep breath and called the doctor.

"Hold on. I'll put Dr. Meyer on the phone." The minutes slowly ticked away as I waited for him to take the phone.

"Hi, Mrs. Gilliam. Well, I stayed up with her until 11 p.m.; there's something special about this dog. She took a turn for the good, and if you would like to come get her, I think she'd recuperate better in a loving home. Give us until around 2:00 p.m. to prepare her to leave."

"Oh yes, thank you, Dr. Meyer; we will go down to pick her up at 3 p.m."

That was the beginning of adventures with Tabitha. I named her Tabitha because in the New Testament book of Acts 9:36–42, it states that Peter prayed for a dead woman named Tabitha, and she came alive. Tabitha received e-mails from the bichon rescue, and her case was discussed in a medical veterinarian handbook for students.

Speaking to a group of women two weeks later, I shared Tabitha's story, "When the odds are against you, ladies, and either you are suffering with a medical issue, relationships, finances, or other, you can come through it and live a better life." Prayer and love can heal the most desperate, hopeless person. Taking time to pray for someone is the most generous and sacrificial gift given to another person.

In the beginning of adjusting to her new environment, one evening Tabitha bit my hand as I started to remove her from our bed. It was deep but didn't require stitches. As my doctor was giving me a tetanus shot, she said, "You better get rid of that dog; she'll probably bite you again." I smiled as I stood up. "No, I cannot do that, and we will be just fine." Giving up on Tabitha was not an option, but working with her by providing consistent, loving boundaries paid off.

Tabitha began to thrive, and that little twenty-four-pound powerhouse must have endured some horrible conditions. When I walked her, she projected herself as the queen of the neighborhood, strutting in her walk and barking at the sight of another dog in a manner that alerted them to her presence. She appeared as though she owned the neighborhood and no one ought to mess with her. At the dog park, Tabitha completely ignored the smaller dogs but ran into the middle of the pack of large dogs and chased them the entire time.

"Hey, what happened to the meat?" I exclaimed as I turned around to see the meat was removed from between my croissant sandwich. I discovered she could steal the meat off your sandwich and leave the bread while you simply turned your head. Her survival skills were incredibly advanced, but she was a caring, loving canine companion.

I brought Tabitha closer and said, "The day you were rescued was the beginning of new life for both of us, Tabitha. I wonder where you've been, what you've seen, and all you've experienced. I'm sorry you suffered so much; you didn't deserve it. I'm protecting you so you never have to experience that kind of pain again. You're a genuine miracle, and I love you so much."

Insight: Have you ever had a pet that you talked to and cried with and that animal helped you express your feelings?

Chapter 9:

Prayer Learned

Staying with Mom and Dale during my first summer break at Evangel University, we read a devotional on prayer. One day Mom said, "When you were four or five, I walked by your room at night, and on occasion I would hear you kissing and spitting. I stopped and asked what you were doing, and you told me you were kissing God and spitting on the devil. I don't know where you got that from, but I was surprised you knew to pray like that." Though Mom pushed us to attend church, we were not taught about prayer, Jesus, or salvation. Perhaps I acquired a vague awareness from the sermons or Sunday school class of God as good and the devil bad. It was a creative means of expressing my emotions; I wonder if it caused God to smile.

A widow named Hazel came periodically to relieve Mom of ironing and to care for my brother and me if we were sick or home from school and needed supervision. Hazel was a polio survivor and had particular difficulty with her right leg when she tried to walk. There were small red acne-like sores on her arms and face, and it caused me not to want her to touch me. Her speech was impeded at times, which may have been a result of polio. Her husband died a couple of years before Mom met her, and her son lived with relatives. At Christmas she made sure Greg and I had a gift from her. It was always a coloring book that had already been used and had a few pages blank to color. At about age eight, I began to pray nightly for

God to heal Mrs. Bessler's leg. I don't know what happened to her after we moved, but I believe my prayers had some positive effect for Hazel Bessler. I understand now when Jesus said in Matthew 18:2–4 in the New English Translation:

"He called a child, had him stand among them, and said, 'I tell you the truth, unless you turn around and become like little children, you will never enter the kingdom of heaven! Whoever then humbles himself like this little child is the greatest in the kingdom of heaven.'"

Jesus' disciples just asked Him who was the greatest in the kingdom of heaven.

Jesus calls the children over and uses the image of humility and of the uncomplicated child-like faith. How and why I prayed for Hazel Bessler's healing at a young age is a mystery to me. As years slipped by, shame, anger, and unworthiness smothered my ability to pray. Pleading for rescue was my only prayer. A simple prayer a child would shout when in urgent need of his or her mother or father. An emphatic shriek for swift help was a frequent prayer I directed toward heaven. Through the years I began to ignore God; however, He never forgot or rejected me.

Waiting in pharmacies for tranquilizers and pain pill prescriptions to be filled was a regular routine at least twice a month or more, along with other drugs.

Preoccupied with putting my hands around the bottle of codeine pills and swallowing a couple, I stood next to a dark-brown-haired woman in her sixties. Twisting and wringing her hands together, she was waiting for medicine for her sick husband.

Nervously she muttered, "Who is going to help me take care of Ed in the afternoon?"

"Excuse me," I said to her. "Is your husband sick?"

"Yes, he had a stroke last month and needs constant care, and I'm not sure how I'm going to do that."

To my astonishment, I blurted out, "If I wasn't sick myself, I would help you, but I'm going to pray for your husband's healing and for strength for you."

A contrived smile hid her pain and fear as she thanked me. The pharmacist called my name as he rang up the sale. I grabbed the small bag and left. Turning the corner, I walked close to the wall and said, "Oh God, please heal this man from the stroke and bring the people needed to take care of him. Give the wife peace and strength. Amen." Did I have the right to pray to the Almighty when I was as estranged from God as anyone? Not sure how that works, but I felt a sense of peace in praying for the woman and her husband.

Walking my IV pole to the solarium at Boca Hospital in Florida, I flopped into an oversized chair and sighed deeply. I saw an older Black woman across from me reading what looked like a Bible. I leaned forward and said, "Excuse me, madam, are you reading the Bible?" "Why yes, I am. Can I help you?" she responded. "My life is a mess, and I'm causing health problems for my mother. She had a seizure today in my hospital room for no apparent reason. I'm scared and can't seem to pull my life together. I'm a drug addict and alcoholic, and I'm in the hospital because my stomach is inflamed due to the pills and alcohol. I wish I could die." "Oh honey, there is help for you in the Lord Jesus Christ. Can I pray for you?" "Oh, please do, my mom's a Christian, and she'd appreciate it also." This tiny ball of fire of a woman stood up and put her hands on my shoulders. She prayed a prayer like I'd never heard before. She was loud but spoke with authority, as though Jesus was her friend and she shared His power. After she completed praying, I looked around to see if anyone was watching, but she didn't care about anyone but me. She took my name and phone number and said she and her sister would pray for Mom and me at their prayer meeting that night. The following day the phone rang, and it was the woman who had prayed. She asked how I was and chatted for a few minutes. Shocked by her concern and care, I couldn't thank her enough. It doesn't matter what church you attend or even if you belong to a community of faith. Whatever culture, tribe, country, age, or experience, if you are a Christian and follow Jesus Christ, you can pray in Jesus' name for anyone and know God hears and responds. Recalling that day was like it was yesterday. I've often thought of that dear woman and given thanks to the Lord, asking Him to bless her. I shall never forget her, but more importantly, God will always remember the hope she gave me that day. That amazing woman integrated her faith into every aspect of her life, unlike some Christians who dichotomize their faith into spiritual exercises like prayer, attending church, tithing side, and other activities. Then there is the unspiritual half of their life that doesn't consider their free time, entertainment and finances, honesty, or integrity as a necessary piece of their faith and worship. Everything

Christians do in life, from how they treat their neighbors to being honest on their income tax filing, is required in order to have a holistic Christian worldview that is appealing and draws others to Christ.

Various Christians believe we should see the results of praying, which mirrors our culture, which measures a person's value and productiveness by the results of the person's work. The woman who prayed for me never saw or knew what became of me, but I believe she understood it didn't matter when and how God answered; she knew her prayers were not in vain.

Our prayers never expire, and though we may not receive the answers we want, God has not forgotten, and His timing is perfect. Over 650 prayers are in the Bible and include prayer for a wife (Genesis 24:12–14), prayer for forgiveness and help (Ezra 5:15), prayer for healing and length of days (Isaiah 38:3), prayer for mercy (Luke 18:13), from Jesus on the cross (Luke 23:24), and many more. God answers prayer however He desires. A common cliché for Christians states that God gives one of three responses: yes, no, or wait. That reply is a general, all-inclusive statement that can be intended to direct a person toward acceptance of one of the three answers. People are complex and at various stages of their faith and can explore the topic of prayer at greater length. Christians should not discontinue learning and reading God's Word about prayer.

I continued to wander in darkness until, finally, at the portals of death, I entered The Walter Hoving Home, a Christian drug and alcohol program. I carried needles and pills and smelled of alcohol when I entered; women sat up with me and prayed through the night as I lay listless on a couch. Some staff feared I might die and suggested medical care as an option. I was informed later that the leadership at The Walter Hoving Home confidently believed if they prayed around the clock, I would survive. By God's grace and mercy, He spared my life and began a transformation process that continues daily. While detoxing, I occupied a bed in one of the girl's rooms; during daylight a couple of staff members took turns sitting with me and praying. At night I was taken downstairs and laid on the couch in the front room while some of the ladies who were close to graduation sat with me and prayed. The Bentons' son, Jim, a guy of large stature, carried me upstairs during the day and brought me down for the nighttime prayer shift.

After days of being semi-comatose, I slowly regained consciousness enough to ask where I was and how I got there. After a short explanation, my memory began to recall the story.

Listening to people pray at mealtime and at prayer meetings became a perpetual occurrence. I did not detect advanced memorization or reading of prayers but people praying from their heart without rehearsal or hesitation. Some recent admissions to the Home refused to pray aloud, and that was acceptable. Prayer flowed more naturally from those who had been walking with Christ for a number of years and exemplified the scripture in 1 Thessalonians 5:17, where Paul implores his readers to "pray without ceasing." Paul means Christians should develop a lifestyle of endless communication with the Lord in their hearts and minds.

No one stood out praying with lofty words or lengthy rhetoric. Praying out loud was not mandatory, but each woman was expected to spend forty-five minutes in quiet devotional time every morning. The only format was to pray and read the Bible or use a Christian devotional. Initially using the word "Father" to describe God was confusing and stirred up internal conflict. Though God could not be compared to my dad, the word "Father" triggered a fearful alarm. Wounds and distrust arising from an abusive relationship with a father can distort a person's view of God, the heavenly Father.

During church services on Sundays and a midweek service on Wednesday nights, prayer and worship could get loud as people raised their hands in an act of surrender and gratitude to God. Some voiced thanks intensely at a passionate volume; others were quieter and prayed on bended knees in a reverent state. Everyone was genuinely thankful for the forgiveness Jesus brought and the release from the sins that kept us bound. God had done for us what we could not do for ourselves...

Psalm 96:3–5 says, "Declare his glory among the nations, his marvelous deeds among all peoples. For great is the Lord and most worthy of praise; he is to be feared above all gods. For all the gods of the nations are idols, but the Lord made the heavens."

Praying includes being honest with the Lord, waiting on Him for answers, and surrendering our expectations to His plan and purposes.

"To one who has faith, no explanation is necessary. To one without faith, no explanation is possible" (Thomas Aquinas, 1225–1274).

My journey into learning and living in the spiritual realm had just started. Understanding God's grace bolstered my intimacy with the Lord and added to overcoming human insecurity in prayer. As I matured in my faith, a passion for pleasing God and not others allowed me to embrace the Holy Spirit and release my fear. As new women came in The Walter Hoving Home, it provided every woman with an opportunity to pray for them. Prayer is one of the most common phenomena for humans and is vital even when it appears God is not answering. It is by faith we live and pray, even when it feels as though God is absent or distant. Feelings are not facts, and we must not let feelings or circumstances dictate our conversations with the Lord. Church history speaks of people of great Christian faith waiting sometimes for years to witness answer to prayer—sometimes not fulfilled in this life.

Communicating with God involves honesty, waiting, and expectations.

- Honesty

A refreshing and vitalizing truth eliminated much pressure when I learned a key component to great prayer is honesty. I understood God knows all things—I mean everything...even a word on my tongue before I say it. We only learn about ourselves as we learn and experience God since He is the giver of life and identity. Timothy Keller says in his book on prayer:

> If God was impersonal, as the Eastern religions teach, then love— something that can happen only between two or more persons— would be an illusion. We can go

> further and say that even if God were only unipersonal,
> then love could not have appeared until after God began
> to create other beings. That would mean Go¹d was more
> fundamentally power than he was love. Love would not
> be as important as power.[xi]

There are days when I pray, and it feels like my words evaporate as soon as they come out of my mouth, that my prayers and conversation with the Lord don't even reach the ceiling. I have prayed for the Lord to change a person I find difficult and challenging. Admitting my attitude and feelings sometimes in anger, I have heard the Lord say, "How about I change you?" When I yield to God, He does take me through a process of change in my heart regarding the person, and I become the beneficiary of the answered prayer.

God desires for us to be honest with Him when we feel He has abandoned us or is unwilling to answer our prayer. Other times we attempt to convince God of how spiritual and deserving we are with counterfeit words and reminders of all we have accomplished in His name. Repenting of pride and self-sufficiency and acknowledging our complete dependence on Him is the only means of pure communion with Him.

Walking at the beach with sunglasses to cover my swollen eyes from crying endlessly throughout the day, I finally accepted and admitted my frustration and disappointment. I'd been praying for several hours after receiving another rejection for a job interview. Months earlier, I had graduated with a doctorate of ministry, and multiple people enthusiastically pronounced that I would have an abundance of job offers. Rejection emails from various churches and ministries I applied at arrived daily. Calls were not returned, and no one was knocking on my door, hopeful they could have me as part of their ministry. Discouraged and distraught, I wanted clarity and direction. I dedicated the day to prayer, but I was continually blurred by tears of letdown and rejection. My pride had been wounded, and I sat humbled in God's presence. Recalling the sacrifices Rick and I gladly made in order to complete the doctorate, I placed myself on the pity pot. It wasn't long before the Lord gently assured me of the rewards of waiting for His plans. The sense of cleansing and closeness to the Lord I felt when I was brutally honest with Him was beneficial.

God's kindness and grace flooded my soul as I ceased complaining and began to worship Him. In a moment of divine enlightenment and silence, I sat in God's presence as though time had halted. "Oh Lord, all I have is this present silent reality with You. I am absorbed in Your presence and fixed in this immediate moment with You. I repent of my attempts to control my destiny, of which my steps You have ordered. I will wait on You with thanksgiving and anticipation." I felt as though time had stopped, and without a word, our union of togetherness spoke clearly. More necessary than finding an answer, that day I was being convinced of the supreme truth that I was loved and known by God.

Later that week I shook my head in disbelief, recognizing how arrogant and puffed up with self-importance I had become. Receiving compliments is affirming, but when you start to believe you are as wonderful as some people pronounce that you are, you are in trouble.

- Waiting

Waiting for God to respond to our prayers, particularly as technology and cultural norms demand and value immediacy, is challenging. The spiritual waiting room is not a time to be passive but a period of learning valuable lessons for the journey ahead.

A popular saying exists that says God answers one of three ways to prayer: yes, no, and wait. Waiting, resting, and remaining in faith while trusting that the Lord is working behind the scenes is key to stability and consistency. Humans are confined to a limited perspective. It's as though an enormous, intricate quit is being unrolled before us. It is a quilt of our life, much that has not yet happened. We only see the details of what is in front of us. On occasion I lay in bed worrying about an incident or about the future when I'm reminded that God never sleeps nor gets weary. So I tell myself, *Give this to the Lord. Go to sleep; He's up all night anyway.*

Trusting, staying in the present, and gratitude create peace. Control is an illusion, and quick fixes are usually ineffective and exhausting.

Second Peter 3:8 (NLT), "But you must not forget this one thing, dear friends: A day is like a thousand years to the Lord, and a thousand years is like a day."

Psalm 27:14 (NLT), "Wait patiently for the Lord. Be brave and courageous. Yes, wait patiently for the Lord."

- Surrendering expectations

Stay in the love of the Father. Feeling we know what would work and how God should answer prayer is common among the human race. Expectations can cause a temper tantrum between you and

God or disappointment and discouragement. We must remember that God's timing, means of answering, and unlimited and unending resources prevail. Faith plays an important role in deferring our will and way to the Lord.

"God, these are innocent little children; why do You allow them to suffer?" The frequent unresolved question of suffering has been asked by masses throughout history. The inability to make sense of pain and suffering, especially to the innocent, has commonly been a deciding factor for a person's view of God. Many resolve the question by believing God is either not all-powerful or not all-good. Suffering is an emotional and illogical dilemma for many. Repeatedly I have commonly been asked from the Christian community, "Why did God allow him or her to suffer so much? She was a faithful believer and served the Lord faithfully." Though a one-size response does not fit all and precise answers are not available, comfort and care apply. The belief that a model Christian should not suffer or is entitled to a more pain-free life is evidence of incorrect theology. Though throughout the Old Testament suffering was viewed as punishment from God, it did not always indicate a lack of faith or displeasure by God. In the book of Job, we see a man and his family lose everything and suffer beyond measure. But Job was not being punished by God but was rewarded for his faithfulness by receiving an abundance of blessings greater than before his suffering.

In the New Testament, the apostle Paul, John the Baptist, and all of the disciples suffered for following Christ. Don't let go of God, just expectations. That does not suggest we should not expect the

Lord to act in our circumstances or to bless us; just remember it is the grace and mercy of God. Past experiences, particularly as a child, where we feel God failed us can return when our loved one died when we prayed continually, the job didn't work out, our child is smoking weed and is in unhealthy relationships, or the rent is raised. As I reflect I understand what I did not comprehend at the time. Expectations accumulate like stains on the back of the neck of our favorite white shirt. If we are not aware on unmet expectations, we can start to resent God or our spouse or the person who is not giving us what we believe he or she should give us. Some of our expectations come from our family of origin and other central relationships.

Our ideal of who God is and what to expect takes time, and it is difficult to accept the real and actual God. But God is so far superior to your expectations you will be unable to express it in words. Maturity in our faith always involves understanding and acceptance of the God who does not fit into our frame of who we think He is. God allows and desires us to be who we are and no one else. We must allow God to be who He is because He will not change His righteous and loving character to make us feel better.

God doesn't care so much about how you pray and what and when.

Prayer can become boring and ritualistic. We can rejuvenate our prayer life by drawing our prayers in circles or doodles and filling in the people or events we are bringing before the Lord.

- Write a letter to God; be brutally honest, and don't dwell on it too long.

189

- Dance your prayer. Put on your favorite worship or other music and dance as an act of worship to God and present your prayers.
- Sing using songs you know or made-up songs.
- Walk or exercise and pray.
- Pray scriptures.

There are bowls in heaven in which our prayers are stored.

> Not one bowl for all of them but "bowls." We don't know how many but I think it very likely that each of us has our own bowl in heaven. I don't know if it's literal or symbolic. It doesn't matter. The principle is still the same. God has something in which He stores our prayers for use at the proper time.[xii]

Revelation 5:8 (NIV), "And when he had taken it, the four living creatures and the twenty-four elders fell down before the Lamb. Each one had a harp and they were holding golden bowls full of incense, which are the prayers of God's people." Revelation 8:3–5 (NIV):

> Another angel, who had a golden censer, came and stood at the altar. He was given much incense to offer, with the prayers of all God's people, on the golden altar in front of the throne. The smoke of the incense, together with the prayers of God's people, went up before God from the angel's hand. Then the angel took the censer, filled it with fire from the altar, and hurled it on the earth; and there came peals of thunder, rumblings, flashes of lightning and an earthquake.

Learning Prayer from Others

Trappist Monk Thomas Merton's prayer from *Thoughts in Solitude*, page 83:

> God, we have no idea where we are going. We do not see the road ahead of us. We cannot know for certain where it will end. Nor do we really know ourselves, and the fact that we think we are following your will does not mean that we are actually doing so.
>
> But we believe that the desire to please you does in fact please you. And we hope we have that desire in all that we are doing. We hope that we will never do anything apart from that desire. And we know that if we do this you will lead us by the right road, though we may know nothing about it. Therefore, we will trust you always though we may seem to be lost and in the shadow of death. We will not fear, for you are ever with us, and you will never leave us to face our perils alone.[xiii]

The prayer said often in Alcoholics Anonymous and other groups is the Serenity Prayer. The full Serenity Prayer was written by Theologian Reinhold Niebuhr, a German pastor and Nazi resister.

The *original* full version by Reinhold Niebuhr (1932–1933):

> God, give us grace to accept with serenity the things that cannot be changed,
> Courage to change the things which should be changed,
> and the wisdom to distinguish the one from the other.
> Living one day at a time, enjoying one moment at a time,
> Accepting hardship as a pathway to peace, taking, as Jesus did, this sinful world as it is,
> Not as I would have it, Trusting that You will make all

things right, If I surrender
to Your will, So that I may be reasonably happy in this life,
And supremely happy with You forever in the next.
Amen.

The Lord's Prayer:

This, then, is how you should pray.
Our Father in heaven, hallowed be your name, your kingdom come,
your will be done, on earth as it is in heaven. Give us today our daily bread.
And forgive us our debts, as we also have forgiven our
debtors
And lead us not into temptation, but deliver us from the
evil one.

The closing sentence, "for thine is the kingdom, and the power, and the glory forever," was added later but is an essential worshipful reading concluding phrase to the prayer.

The Lord's Prayer in Matthew 6:5–15 is included in a section of the Sermon on the Mount where Jesus talks about prayer. He warns against not praying in public with the motivation of being heard and gaining attention and being esteemed as spiritual. Jesus also instructs His followers not to pray pagan prayers designed to manipulate all pagan gods.

Prayers manufactured by formulas, no matter how sincere, do not promote an honest and surrendered relationship with God. Jesus chose the bullion nuggets of the Christian faith to include in instructing His disciples to pray based on an intimate relationship with God the Father.

People tend to repeat the Lord's Prayer in a mechanical manner due to the frequency of hearing it and repeating it.

This prayer solidifies my entrance at salvation into the family of God, as Jesus begins with "our Father." He does not say the father, my father, or your father but "our Father in heaven."

Romans 8:29 (NIV) states, "For those God foreknew he also predestined to be conformed to the image of his Son, that he might be the firstborn among many brothers and sisters." Hebrews 2:11 (NIV) says:

"Both the one who makes people holy and those who are made holy are of the same family. So, Jesus is not ashamed to call them brothers and sisters." One of the most notable to me is the passage in Matthew 12:46–50 (NIV), where Jesus publicly describes His genuine family.

The scripture says:

> While Jesus was still talking to the crowd, his mother and brothers stood outside, wanting to speak to him. Someone told him, "Your mother and brothers are standing outside, wanting to speak to you." He replied to him, "Who is my mother, and who are my brothers?" Pointing to his disciples, he said, "Here are my mother and my brothers. For whoever does the will of my Father in heaven is my brother and sister and mother."

The next part of the prayer declares the Father's characteristic that we, His children, should acknowledge and respect. "Hallowed or holy is your name." Knowing who God the Father is and who allows us to pray. "Thy kingdom come and thy will be done." No longer our kingdom or our will but God's rule over our lives, but as kingdom citizens, our lives demand kingdom living.

After affirming God's rule over all, including our lives, the prayer rotates to our needs. "Give us this day our daily bread." Praying for the Lord to "give us" our daily bread indicates our reliance on Him as our provider and source. I recall the children in the wilderness who daily needed to depend on God's provisions for food (Exodus 16). The word "bread" in the prayer is pregnant with meaning. It means daily sustenance of life-sustaining food but can also be used in a metaphorical means to whatever is needed to strengthen, support, and produce salvation. There have been times I have prayed for daily courage, compassion, forgiveness, and grace as part of my daily bread. On occasion I have wanted tomorrow's bread today, uncomfortable with taking life one day at a time. "Just tell me today, Lord, what is going to emerge in this situation so I can better prepare." I can make provision without knowing the outcome. Usually I hear only silence and a sense of trusting my tomorrows with Him.

Confession of our sin and receiving forgiveness are paramount in preserving our relationship with the Lord and deepening the level of intimacy. Jesus made forgiveness a priority knowing that unconfessed sin and resentment against others are poison to our entire being. Unworthy as we are, God, in His mercy and compassion, forgives us when we ask, but completely forgiving others is often a process we resist. Unknowingly we say we forgive the person but have not gone through the steps. It is usually more time-consuming and may involve feeling the hurt behind the resentment. I have asked the Lord before, "Give me the willingness to forgive because, in my own strength and compassion, I cannot." Sometimes God allows us to see the person(s) as He sees them, separating the deed from the person. We can achieve full forgiveness if we desire it.

There have been times I have experienced the church as a group of nice angry people. The next two phrases recognize the need for the Lord's protection walking into temptation and give Him permission to lead us away from the potential mess we may be ready to encounter. To deliver us from evil is another part of the prayer, which asks to be led out of evil when we are ignorant or unable to leave on our own. Evil disguises itself, and we can be deceived, but giving God authority to deliver us even when we do not see the evil means we walk by faith and not by sight. I've known of people who, while walking down the aisle to get married, were clearly told by the Holy Spirit not to proceed with the ceremony. Some people listened and aborted the wedding, while others did what they wanted to do.

The Lord's Prayer and each of the prayers I have shared are about relationships. Answers to prayer are discovered now and then as we wrestle to understand God in our communion with Him. Prayer is about relationship in its healthiest and most desirable state. Prayer doesn't necessarily provide a less busy life, but it does offer a less busy heart and mind.

When Jesus describes the intimacy He desires with us, He talks about joining us for dinner. He states in Revelation 3:20 (ESV), "Behold, I stand at the door and knock. If anyone hears my voice and opens the door, I will come in to him and eat with him, and he with me."

Chapter 10:

Conclusion

Learning to Float

Throughout my adolescent and teenage years and into adulthood, I practiced to become a better swimmer. Nothing feels as refreshing as plunging into a crystal clear pool on a humid summer day or feeling the force of ocean waves flooding over you. I recall having a swimming lesson in school and wanting to make the swim team, putting time and energy into utilizing my legs and arms to improve my skill. Not good enough to make the swim team, I persisted in getting better. In my late forties, I started to participate in water aerobics classes and spent most of my time in the pool exercising. But swimming never quite flowed for me; either my breathing or arm and leg coordination was off. It's as though I was fighting the water with intensity and normally ran out of energy before reaching my goal. On one occasion I was attempting to do a backstroke but became frightened and started trashing about as I protected myself from getting water in my nose and mouth. Trying to swim well had become a task, so I spent time exercising in the water. Then I heard an internal voice say, "Why don't you just relax and float?" Thinking I must be mistaken because I didn't know how to float, I smiled and kept doing jumping jacks. Again, I heard, "Just lie back in the water slowly and gently—let your limbs and head relax." With my feet barely touching the bottom of the pool, I stood still and gradually tilted my body back. I panicked the first two or three attempts, but

197

steadily I lay on my back, gradually and meticulously placing my head in the water as though it were made of thin *papier-mâché*. Looking up at the clear blue sky with various shaped white clouds seemed to calm me. In a mental recollection, I remember watching adults teaching their toddlers to swim by first holding their back and head as they learn to float. It shifts into a trust issue—calm enough to trust the person keeping your head above water. Resisting the urge to panic and flail my arms and legs, I remained tranquil. The longer I stayed in that position, the easier it was to enjoy the moment.

Though floating in water may not seem like a meaningful accomplishment to most people, I learned fundamental lessons about myself that I will never forget. Time after time, I relied on myself to win the battles of life. Fiercely fighting for success, recognition, and, most critically, love, I gave up and self-medicated my failures and emptiness with substances and behaviors, learning that being a Christian does not mean just believing in Jesus Christ and all will be well. But bolstered and empowered by the Holy Spirit and His Word, I know God goes before me and gives priority to my cultivating a relationship with Him. Fear can no longer fuel my ambitions and choices or steal my energy. Based on the confident trust of my relationship with the Lord that He initiated with me, I realize surrendering to His care and direction preserves my strength and passion for fulfilling His will for me and brings me joy. Trusting that the Lord has my back and is guiding me with every breath allows me to float even in times of uncertainty and suffering. And chaos.

Being in control is just an illusion, and whenever I start to fear or panic, I visualize God holding me up and instructing me to relax and remain in the moment. Challenges and conflicts continue to demand my time and energy, but I am shortening the time I allow circumstances or people to overwhelm me. When I exercise the visual experience of floating with the Lord at my side, I feel muscles loosen and calmness guard my entire being, peacefully trusting Him. I can now relish being in the water and spending time just floating. Jesus invites me to relinquish the reins of my life and the desperate striving to bring change to situations and people out of my control. Time in communion with the Father is the ultimate means of reordering life. Numerous times it is me that needs the change, either of attitude or perspective. Accepting that God has created me in His image with all my limitations, failures, and doubts is the beginning of greater acceptance of the unexpected disappointments and hurts of life. Next time you are frenzied by troubles, emotions that feel too overwhelming, or disillusioned with life, try floating. Not only will God hold you so you become secure, but He will order your steps and float past the chaotic splashing around you. Jesus says in John 4:13–14 (NIV), "Jesus answered, 'Everyone who drinks this water will be thirsty again, but whoever drinks the water I give them will never thirst. Indeed, the water I give them will become in them a spring of water welling up to eternal life.'" God's love produces healing that is transformational when we present our uncovered heart, soul, and mind in all their vulnerability.

There are times I still feel as though I'm in a pot of stew with faith and doubt, love and fear, and selfishness and sacrifice for others.

These contrary emotions exist for all Christians at times, but they don't signify we don't love the Lord or are not following Him. Just as there was more to "Doubting Thomas" than his label, there are times we struggle with our faith (John 20:19–23).

Early in my pastorate, I was introduced to a woman named Cora Maltby, who was homebound most of the time, caring for the needs of her two bedridden daughters suffering from Huntington's disease. Huntington's is a rare, inherited disease that causes the progressive breakdown of nerve cells in the brain. There is not a cure for Huntington's, and symptoms cannot be maintained. It is a horrendous progressive illness that evidently renders a person unable to move, speak, swallow, and evidently die. Tube feeding of patients with Huntington's can extend their life by not dying of starvation or dehydration. When I entered the process, both daughters had been incapacitated for ten years or more.

Taking a deep breath, I knocked on the door of the Maltby home. Not looking forward to seeing the two daughters in bed with the disease, I thanked God for the compassion and opportunity to minister to Cora and the girls. I entered Judy's room, and, looking down at her thin body with hands and legs stiffened from the disease, I greeted her. "Hi Judy, I'm here to pray with you. I know you miss going to church, and I'm the new pastor, Barbara Gilliam." Her ability to make eye contact had been ravished by the disease, and she lay there unresponsive. She was a pretty lady with soft brown hair and eyes. I whispered to God in a rather demanding and questionable manner, "Why don't You heal these girls or take them to heaven,

Lord? You used them at church; they were married at one time and able to help others; now they cannot even help themselves."

But as each set of fingerprints is different, every person has a distinct, individual purpose. God did not design us to be carbon copies. Being deeply rooted in your unique self is something the Lord desires. I was superficial as I questioned God with arrogance and disrespect, questioning his reasons for allowing this suffering to continue.

Distinctly and without question, the Lord replied, "Barbara, there are people walking around appearing successful and well who are much more disabled than these two girls." Still reflecting on God's gracious response, I repented and continued to grasp the truth that only God puts value on every person He has designed. Judy and Karen are of no less value as the disease progresses, and no human understands what occurs in the spiritual realm on a daily basis for Judy and Karen. Honored to officiate at different times at both of the girls' funerals, I discovered a number of people sprinkled around the country who were inspired and encouraged by Karen and Judy's courage and tenacity to continue to serve God through the various stages of the disease. Judy and Karen were undeterred by a painful disease that stole their lives. The girls and Cora lived to believe and accept God's unique purpose for their lives.

Labeling others as of little worth based on their ability to produce and perform or their outward demeanor is contrary to the biblical appraisement and is not pleasing to the Lord. When God was selecting a king to replace Saul, He said to Samuel the Prophet,

"Do not consider his appearance or his height, for I have rejected him. The Lord does not look at the things people look at. People look at the outward appearance, but the Lord looks at the heart" (1 Samuel 16:7, NIV). In John 7:24 (NIV), Jesus said, "Stop judging by mere appearances, but instead judge correctly." Often I have imagined people with a label across their foreheads that reads, "Handle with care. I'm made in the image of God." "Because we are an envisioning lifeform, we cannot remain neutral and either we reflect the Creator or someone or something created."[xiv]

Creation is a surge of God's love in all of its creativity, assortment, and grandeur. God did not hold back when sharing His cosmos. Someone once said how dull life would be if God only used black and white in forming the universe. As humans made in the image of God, we possess the gift of being awakened to God's unconditional love that accepts us as we are with no strings attached. Our personal relationship with the Lord bulldozes out our fears and isolation and fills the hallow crevices with holy love.

I cannot know myself without knowing God. There have been numerous periods of time I've experienced my internal reality quite different than the external appearance projected to others. These are experiences of enlightenment for me and force a deeper self-awareness and responsibility to examine my motives. When you ask God for His perspective and wisdom, He may reveal some insecurities or failed expectations.

Only God undisputedly knows us and loves us deeply, including the parts of us we are not yet mindful of. When we understand

and accept that nothing will separate us from God's love, endless transformation can happen.

"If you do not tell the truth about yourself you cannot tell it about other people" (Virginia Woolf).

Yearning for meaning and influence by worshipping the idols of this world will never compare to the actualization of our relationship with God.

By not accepting who God has created, we cause a silent hemorrhaging of the soul. As the layers are peeled away, we find our genuine self and our truth, which no longer is hidden, and over time we cease avoiding it. We all have a dark side we try to run from and bury, but once you find beauty in what you perceive as the ugliness, you are less likely to reject it.

Though pursuing wholeness is a life-long progression, accepting our darkened, masked part is a primary first step. Our shadow side includes our past experiences that have shaped who we are, and in many cases it is full of shame. If we ignore these unresolved potential minefields, we may not recognize unhealthy patterns of decision-making and relationships. Incorporating all aspects of ourselves with the love of Christ restores harmony and promotes acceptance.

Someone once advised against comparing, saying, "It is not your race and not your pace." Comparing yourself with others can result in anxiety and unrealistic expectations. I've had multiple role models who I admired and respected, but I learned I could not emulate or copy them—just take the good attributes and make them mine.

An internal sanctuary of belonging in your soul is the place where God rules and rests with you.

Our identity is a discovery over a period of time that we are sealed with the Holy Spirit as a deposit of the good things to come. Knowing God and knowing ourselves is part of the transformational knowledge of accepting the unique and magnificent person He intended us to be. Transformational knowledge is always personal and occurs in relationship.

Every human being is created in the image of God regardless of appearance, place of origin, abilities, or behavior and is equally loved by God. I cannot know myself without knowing God. When the contrast between who I project myself to be outwardly and my genuine internal reality is wide, I must take time to evaluate my level of self-awareness and what is motivating me. All people hope for approval from others and crave belonging. Only God knows us on a level even we don't know and utter adores and loves us more completely. As the layers are peeled away, you will find your authentic self and your personal truth, which no longer needs to be hidden.

My hope and prayer is that these writings will help you recognize and experience the unconditional love of God.

When you read my experiences of grappling hopelessly in darkness while searching for a purpose, you will know that regardless of how you have lived, God will never leave you alone or reject you. The invisible but ingrained words on your forehead that say, "Handle with care, for I am created in the image of God," will remain forever.

Grab Jesus' nailed-scarred hand. He is reaching out to you and will not let go. You belong in the family of God.

Welcome home!

Psalm 23:6 (NLT), "Surely your goodness and unfailing love will pursue me all the days of my life, and I will live in the house of the Lord forever."

Contact Information

Barbara L. Gilliam
7924 Alhambra Drive
Huntington Beach, CA
714.404.2291
Vendors@CompassionateWisdomWorks.org
barb@barbgilliam.com

Endnotes

[i] *Introduction*

David G. Benner, *The Gift of Being Yourself: The Sacred Call to Self-Discovery* (Downers Grove: IVP Books, 2004), 61.

Chapter 2: When Did It Begin?

[ii] W. Ross Hastings, "The Trinity and Human Sexuality: Made in the Image of the Triune God," *CRUX* 54.2 (Summer 2018): 10–24, 47.

Chapter 5: Oh, What a Tangled Web We Weave When First We Practice to Deceive

[iii] Henry Cloud and John Townsend, *Boundaries: When to Say Yes, How to Say No to Take Control of Your Life* (Grand Rapids: Zondervan, 1992), 31.

Chapter 6: Addiction

[iv] "Overdose Death Rates," National Institute on Drug Abuse, last modified January 20, 2022, https://www.drugabuse.gov/drug-topics/trends-statistics/overdose-death-rates.

[v] "Marijuana Use and Your Health," Colorado Environmental Public Health Tracking, accessed 2022, https://coepht.colorado.gov/marijuana-use-and-your-health.

"The Negative Health Effects of Marijuana Use," Get Smart about Drugs, last updated November 4, 2021, https://www.getsmartaboutdrugs.gov/content/negative-health-effects-marijuana-use.

"Know the Risks of Marijuana," SAMHSA, last updated July 28, 2022, https://www.samhsa.gov/marijuana.

[vi] "Proverbs 10," http://www.sermonseeds.org/Poetry/Proverbs/Proverbs%2010.htm.

[vii] James Maxey, "The power of Words in Mark: Their Potential and their Limits," *Currents in Theology and Mission* 37, n. 4 (August 2021): 302.

[viii] Brennan Manning, *The Furious Longing of God* (Colorado Springs: David C. Cook Publishing, 2009), 34–35, Kindle.

[ix] Ibid., 18.

Chapter 7: Choose Life or Death

[x] Claudia Black, "It Will Never Happen to Me," accessed 2021, video, 57:59, https://video.search.yahoo.com/search/video?fr=yfp-t-s&ei=UTF8&p=clau dia+black+it+will+never+happen+to+me+video+youtube#id=1&vid=ae652 3dad466d80fc40faab7b52c9704&action=click.

Chapter 9: Prayer Learned

[xi] Timothy Keller. *Prayer: Experiencing Awe and Intimacy with God* (New York: Penguin Publishing Group, 2014), 50–51, Kindle.

[xii] Dutch Sheets. *Intercessory Prayer: How God Can Use Your Prayers to Move Heaven and Earth.*

[xiii] Thomas Merton, *Thoughts in Solitude* (New York: Farrar, Straus and Giroux, 1956), 83.

Chapter 10: Conclusion

[xiv] G. K. Beale, *We Become What We Worship: A Biblical Theology of Idolatry* (Downers Grove: IVP Academic, 2008), 110–111, Kindle.

Bibliography

Beale, G. K. *We Become What We Worship: A Biblical Theology of Idolatry.* Downers Grove: IVP Academic, 2008. Kindle.

Benner, David G. *Surrender to Love: Discovering the Heart of Christian Spirituality.* Downers Grove: IVP Books, 2003, 79.

———. *The Gift of Being Yourself: The Sacred Call to Self-Discovery.* Downers Grove: IVP Books, 2004.

Black, Claudia. "It Will Never Happen to Me." Accessed 2021. Video, 57:59. https://video.search.yahoo.com/search/video?fr=yfp-t-s&ei=UTF8&p=claudia+black+it+will+never+happen+to+me+video+youtube#id=1&vid=ae6523dad466d80fc40faab7b52c9704&action=click.

Cloud, Henry and John Townsend. *Boundaries: When to Say Yes, How to Say No to Take Control of Your Life.* Grand Rapids: Zondervan, 1992.

Colorado Environmental Public Health Tracking. "Marijuana Use and Your Health." Accessed 2022. https://coepht.colorado.gov/marijuana-use-and-your-health.

Get Smart about Drugs. "The Negative Health Effects of Marijuana Use." Last updated November 4, 2021. https://www.getsmartaboutdrugs.gov/content/negative-health-effects-marijuana-use.

Hastings, W. Ross. "The Trinity and Human Sexuality: Made in the Image of the Triune God." *CRUX* 54.2 (Summer 2018): 10–24, 47.

Keller, Timothy. *Prayer: Experiencing Awe and Intimacy with God.* New York: Penguin Publishing Group, 2014. Kindle.

Macchia, Stephen A. *Crafting a Rule of Life: An Invitation to the Well-Ordered Way.* Downers Grove: Zondervan, 2012, 13–14, 91.

Manning, Brennan. *The Furious Longing of God.* Colorado Springs: David C. Cook Publishing, 2009. Kindle.

Maxey, James. "The power of Words in Mark: Their Potential and their Limits." *Currents in Theology and Mission* 37, n. 4 (August 2021): 302.

Merton, Thomas. *Thoughts in Solitude.* New York: Farrar, Straus and Giroux, 1956.

National Institute on Drug Abuse. "Overdose Death Rates." Last modified January 20, 2022. https://www.drugabuse.gov/drug-topics/trends-statistics/overdose-death-rates.

Nelson, Richard D. *The Old Testament: Canon, History and Literature.* Nashville: Abingdon Press, 2019, 99–100.

"Proverbs 10." http://www.sermonseeds.org/Poetry/Proverbs/Proverbs%2010.htm.

SAMHSA. "Know the Risks of Marijuana." Last updated July 28, 2022. https://www.samhsa.gov/marijuana.

Sheets, Dutch. *Intercessory Prayer: How God Can Use Your Prayers to Move Heaven and Earth.*

CPSIA information can be obtained
at www.ICGtesting.com
Printed in the USA
BVHW030841060223
657963BV00015B/1155